RUGBY LEAG

CW00746944

IN THE
80s

RUGBY LEAGUE JOURNAL
PUBLISHING

Volume Five in the 'Rugby League Journal History Series'

Ellery Hanley - the first British winner of the Golden Boot award in 1989.
The worldwide award was created by 'Open Rugby' magazine in 1985.

**First published in Great Britain in 2014 by
Rugby League Journal Publishing
P.O.Box 22, Egremont, Cumbria, CA23 3WA**

ISBN 978-09548355-9-0

**Written, edited and designed by Harry Edgar
Marketing and promotion by Ruth Edgar
Printed by The Firpress Group Limited**

Front cover pictures:
Ellery Hanley playing for Great Britain on the 1984 Lions tour.
(Insets) Mal Meninga, Peter Sterling, Andy Gregory and Brett Kenny.
Frontispiece picture:
Garry Schofield's joy at scoring a try in his debut Ashes Test in Sydney in 1984.
(All photos by Andrew Varley)

RUGBY LEAGUE JOURNAL
PUBLISHING

**P.O. Box 22, Egremont, Cumbria, CA23 3WA
E-Mail: rugbyleague.journal@sky.com   Telephone: 01946 811005**
www.rugbyleaguejournal.net

CONTENTS

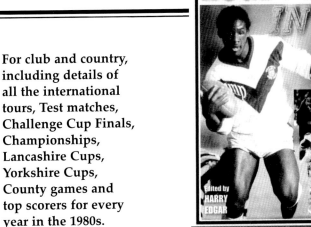

For club and country, including details of all the international tours, Test matches, Challenge Cup Finals, Championships, Lancashire Cups, Yorkshire Cups, County games and top scorers for every year in the 1980s.

Rugby League Journal History Series

(Above) The magic of cup rugby as Alan Hodkinson captained Barrow to the Lancashire Cup in 1983. *(Right)* Eric 'guru' Grothe, a never-to-be-forgotten star of the 1982 Kangaoos who changed the game forever. *(Below)* Ellery Hanley, who became Britain's leading player of the 'eighties.

Thanks

The Publisher would like to extend very special thanks to the photographers Andrew Varley and Eddie Whitham, whose skills have provided so many of the fine images you will see in this book. Other pictures have been taken from the files of the former 'Open Rugby' magazine, and our thanks are extended to the numerous other contributing photographers of the 1980s, notably Eddie Rolmanis. Including so many old pictures means it is often difficult to ascertain their origins, thus there has been no intention to breach anybody's copyright.

5 Governing the game
6 The top club teams
8 The Magnificent Test matches
10 Rugby League Superstars
11 Life in the Second Division
12 Timelines of the decade begin
32 Wakefield Trinity and the greats
34 Lions on tour in 1984
36 Great Britain in the 1980s colour pictures
38 Lions on tour in 1988
41 Great Britain's young hopefuls
42 Great Britain's revival in the '80s
44 European internationals
45 French Tests for Great Britain
46 The 1982 Kangaroos on tour
48 The 1986 Kangaroos on tour
50 The Kiwis on tour
54 The World Cup
55 American Dreams in Milwaukee
56 The World Club Challenge
58 The new clubs explosion
62 County matches - the War of the Roses
65 Rugby Union internationals into League
66 Challenge Cup Finals
70 Championship winners
72 Second Division Championship winners
74 Premiership Finals
78 Lancashire Cup Finals
82 Yorkshire Cup Finals
86 John Player Trophy Finals
90 The game in Australia
92 The game in France
94 The Amateur game
96 The Final Whistle

INTRODUCTION

This is the fifth volume in our *'Rugby League Journal History Series'* as we take you back to the 1980s. Following the same format as our previous volumes on the 'fifties, 'sixties and 'seventies, our aim is to provide easy to read and well illustrated guides to the game's history, providing nostalgia for people old enough to remember those times and some new knowledge for younger generations.

(Above)
**Hussein M'Barki celebrates scoring a try for Fulham.
He was one of the most unique characters who made quite a contribution to Rugby League throughout the 1980s after first being attracted to join Fulham as their first overseas signing.
A former captain of the Moroccan Rugby Union team, he went on to play for several other clubs, among them: Warrington, Hull and Oldham, before returning to Fulham.**

The 'eighties was an incredibly exciting time for Rugby League, one where changes came so rapidly and so positively that the possibilities for the game seemed endless. In Britain, Australia and New Zealand (and even in Papua New Guinea) the game picked itself up after a difficult start to the decade to make remarkable progress. In 1980 nobody could have predicted that, before the decade was out, Rugby League in both Britain and New Zealand would be attracting such huge television audiences and be able to attract record crowds of around 50,000 to international matches, whilst in Australia the annual interstate series would become such a massive sporting and commercial juggernaut with Tina Turner promoting the ever expanding NSW premiership. Among the game's established nations, only in France was Rugby League going backwards, unable to overcome the media backlash from the terrible damage done by its abandoned Championship Final in 1981.

It is impossible to consider the history of British Rugby League in the 'eighties without recognising the massive influence of two key events: the 1982 Kangaroo tour, which changed forever the way the game on the field was played; and the tragedy of the Bradford fire in 1985, which led to stringent new ground safety regulations having a major impact on the financial viability of many clubs. Another new burden the clubs had to come to terms with in the latter part of the decade was the introduction of the so-called 'freedom of contract' system which allowed players to move more freely between clubs and demand much higher payments for their services.

The game itself changed after the 1982 Kangaroos were quickly followed by rule changes in 1983 which saw the ball handed over after the sixth tackle instead of a scrum - this led to a faster game of far less scrums, more tactical kicking and the ball in play for longer; in addition both the 'head' and 'feed' at the scrum was given to the 'non offending side', which further streamlined the game, and helped produce the magnificent contests - at both club and international levels - which put Rugby League on such a pedestal in the second half of the 'eighties.

Throughout that decade I was privileged to be closely involved in many of the game's developments and adventures, and witnessed first hand most of those pivotal events, in my role as publisher of *'Open Rugby'* magazine. I hope you will enjoy sharing some of my memories of them in this book.

Harry Edgar (Editor - 'Rugby League Journal')

GOVERNING THE GAME

During the 1980s the Rugby Football League adapted very successfully to the changing times as a new commercialism came into the game, prompted largely by the acceptance of sponsorship as an integral part of professional sport and the vital importance of television contracts. Ably guided by secretary-general David Oxley throughout the decade, Rugby League's sponsorship portfolio was expertly handled by public relations officer David Howes. It was an era when sponsorship by tobacco companies and breweries was commonplace in major sports, and Rugby League enjoyed significant financial benefits from such associations.

The RFL also expanded its staff significantly when Roland Davis was appointed as its first full time Finance Officer. As well as handling the League's day to day financiall affairs, Roland played a very important role as business manager of the 1984 Lions touring team. After the financially disastrous 1979 tour, the RFL took the wise decision to appoint one of their own full-time employees to oversee the finances of the British touring team and, thanks to Roland's diligence, the 1984 tour turned over a very healthy profit despite the attendances being lower than on the 1979 tour when

(Above) **Mal Meninga lifts the Premiership trophy after inspiring St.Helens to victory on a great day for Rugby League at Elland Road on 11th May 1985 - but just a few miles away at Bradford, a tragedy was unfolding which would, subsequently, have a major effect on Rugby League clubs.**

(Above) **David Oxley, secretary-general of the RFL, pictured in 1986.**

such a major loss occurred. The RFL maintained this successful policy by appointing employee David Howes to be business manager of the 1988 Lions tour.

Commercially, Rugby League built itself up into a very strong state as the decade progressed. As well as sponsorship, big games began to attract vastly increased attendances. The British game had to be grateful to the Australians for much of this thanks to the impact made by the 1982 and 1986 Kangaroos, along with the star quality of many Aussies who came to play for British clubs, but it was the masterstroke of taking big games back to major soccer stadiums (beginning with the 1982 Cup Final replay at Elland Road) which generated much more revenue thanks to their bigger capacities and vastly

(Above) **Reg Parker, a popular Chairman of the RFL in 1984-85.**

increased number of seats. The RFL Council had some excellent Chairmen during the 1980s, most notably Reg Parker in 1984-85, who was always encouraging of new developments in the game whilst always being acutely aware of the difficulties faced by clubs at the lower end of the professional game. No issue became of greater concern than that of ground safety regulations in the aftermath of the tragic fire at Bradford City's Valley Parade in 1985. Some clubs were unable to cope with the pressures placed on them, notably Mr. Parker's own club Blackpool Borough, who were forced to move out of their ground in 1987 - whilst by the end of the decade both York and Hull K.R. would also have to leave their old homes.

CHAIRMEN OF THE RFL

1978-80	Sumner Baxendale (*Wigan*)
1980-81	Jack Myerscough (*Leeds*)
1981-82	Bill Oxley (*Barrow*)
1982-83	Jack Grindrod (*Rochdale H.*)
1983-84	Jack Bateman (*Swinton*)
1984-85	Reg Parker (*Blackpool Boro.*)
1985-86	Joe Seddon (*St.Helens*)
1986-87	David Wigham (*Whitehaven*)
1987-93	Bob Ashby (*Featherstone R.*)

THE TOP CLUB TEAMS

T he 1980s began with the power base in British Rugby League firmly established on the eastern seaboard in the city of Hull, where both clubs dominated the game financially with their big crowds fuelling an ambition to attract top players and win trophies. Both **Hull** and **Hull K.R.** set new transfer fee records for the game by signing Trevor Skerrett and George Fairbairn in 1980 and '81 respectively, and both were first into the overseas market to recruit members of the popular 1980 Kiwi touring team. The Boulevard was brightened up by the presence of Kemble, Leuluai and O'Hara (and, later, Ah Kuoi), whilst in the east of the city at Craven Park the Rovers fans loved the exploits of Prohm, Broadhurst and Gordon Smith. Likewise when the ban on signing Australian players was lifted in 1983, the Hull clubs wasted no time in bringing over some of the Aussie game's top players, including Peter Sterling and John Muggleton to the 'Airlie Birds' and John Dorahy and Gavin Miller to the 'Robins'.

Hull K.R., with Roger Millward as coach, had already tasted Championship success in the late 'seventies, but neighbours Hull F.C. made a remarkably rapid rise from the Second Division in 1978-79 to the point where they were the game's biggest crowd pullers just three years later with an average home league attendance of 13,190 in 1981-82. By 1983 they were the Championship winners and had an impressive record of appearing in three of the decade's first four Challenge Cup Finals, winning the trophy in 1982 in a replay at Elland Road on a magical night for the game. Not to be outdone by their local rivals, Hull K.R. won back-to-back Championships in 1984 and '85 and were widely recognised as a major driving force in the British game.

Meanwhile, the major challengers to this Humberside dominance were **Widnes**, who had been one of the game's most successful clubs in the 1970s and maintained that status throughout the '80s. The Chemics began the decade with two more Challenge Cups in four years and two Premiership titles, and by the end of the 1980s found themselves winning successive Championships and being crowned World Club Champions. The coaching baton passed from Vince Karalius to Doug Laughton, and the Chemics built a wonderfully entertaining team with a perfect combination of local boys and big names from Rugby Union, all held together with overseas grit and experience from the likes of captain Kurt Sorensen, Joe Grima and Phil McKenzie.

Going toe-to-toe with Widnes in the latter years of the '80s were **Wigan**, back at the top in Rugby League after a barren era for one of the most famous clubs in the game. Wigan had begun the decade in the Second Division, and suffered the indignity of being walloped by Fulham in their debut match at Craven Cottage in 1980. Desperate to restore the glory days to Central Park, a new streamlined four-man Board of Directors, headed by Jack Robinson and Maurice Lindsay, managed to get Wigan moving upwards - an early taste of success came with Alex Murphy as coach when the John Player Trophy was won in 1983, followed by a disappointing defeat to Widnes at Wembley in 1984. A year later the Challenge Cup came back to Wigan after a gap of 20 years, with joint coaches Alan McInnes and Colin Clarke at the helm, and then

(Above)
Gary Prohm in the classic attacking style which became so familiar to Hull K.R. fans in the 'eighties as the Robins won two consecutive Championships in 1984 and '85. The New Zealander Prohm had come to prominence on the 1980 Kiwi tour, and proved to be one of the best signings the Hull Kingston Rovers club ever made.

(Left)
Tommy Martyn on the attack for Leigh at Hilton Park against Bradford Northern. Tommy was a key man in Leigh's Championship title winning season of 1981-82, in which he played 40 games, as the side coached by Alex Murphy won Leigh's first Championship for 76 years.

things really took off at Central Park when the New Zealander Graham Lowe came in as coach in 1986 and stars like Hanley, Lydon and Gregory were recruited. In Lowe's first season, Wigan won the Championship for the first time since 1960, and began a run of Challenge Cup wins in 1988 which would go on to break all records and take them well into the next decade.

For two of the game's biggest clubs, **Leeds** and **St.Helens**, the 1980s was a decade without any Challenge Cup or Championship wins - although both managed a John Player Trophy success and Saints enjoyed their one glorious season with Mal Meninga in their ranks as the mighty Australian centre powered them to both the Premiership title and Lancashire Cup in 1984-85.

The one club who really broke the mould in the 'eighties was **Halifax**, taking everyone by surprise as they came from the depths of the Second Division and several very difficult years, to take the game by storm with a Championship and two Wembley Finals in three consecutive seasons. Halifax were promoted from the Second Division in 1984 and just two years later were the Rugby League Champions. Their revival was inspired by President David Brook who recuited 1982 Kangaroo tourist Chris Anderson as player-coach, and a handful of young Australians - who mixed well with the local players to produce some thrilling times at Thrum Hall. And there were other cinderella stories come true as a couple of the underdogs really did have their day when **Leigh** won the Championship in 1982, and **Featherstone Rovers** the Challenge Cup in 1983. Both clubs showed that teams largely made up of local boys could outshine the expensively assembled Humberside giants of the time, and **Castleford** followed their example by winning the Challenge Cup in 1986. As a sign of the changing times in Rugby League, the glamour side of the previous decade, **Salford**, were now well away from the limelight and prolific trophy winners **Warrington**, although always strong challengers, found themselves often missing out during the 'eighties, despite winning a John Player Trophy in 1981 and Premiership title in 1986.

(Above)
Halifax players chair Chris Anderson after he announced his retirement as a player in 1988 after bringing Championship and Challenge Cup glory to Thrum Hall in the mid 'eighties.

(Left)
Mike Coulman in action for Salford in 1982. Coulman had been a star in the Red Devils' glory years in the previous decade, and brought his career to a close as Salford faded from the top.

THE MAGNIFICENT TESTS

(Right)
One of the decade's most dramatic moments, which came in the last minute of the third Test between Great Britain and New Zealand at Elland Road in 1985. Everyone in the stadium held their breath as Lee Crooks took this penalty shot from near the touch-line - his kick was successful, allowing the British to achieve a 6-all draw and level the series with the Kiwis.

(Above)
Deryck Fox, one of the several BARLA 'Young Lions' of 1983 who went on to win full Test honours. Scrum-half Fox was a key player in the Great Britain teams which played the Kiwis in 1985 and the Kangaroos in 1986.

Every year of the 1980s saw international tours taking place and Test matches played, many of which produced some of the classic moments which will be remembered forever in Rugby League's history. Here are some of those Tests we saw which hold some of the most special memories:

1981 - Stade Velodrome, Marseille - France 19, Gt.Britain 2.
It was not one of Great Britain's finest hours, but wonderful to see a Test match back in the city of Marseille, at the famous Velodrome where packed 30,000 plus crowds had provided the backdrop for much of French Rugby League's golden age after the war. Only around 6,000 spectators were scattered around the huge old stadium on this occasion five days before Christmas in 1981, but they saw what would becoming an increasingly rare convincing victory for France, which included two classic winger's tries by Patrick Solal before he was stretchered off with concussion.

1982 - Boothferry Park, Hull - Great Britain 4, Australia 40.
A real landmark moment in sporting history, the day British Rugby League realised the Australians were doing something different. Plenty of clues had already been offered in the third Test in 1978 and the 1979 Ashes series, but some had still refused to get the message. As Max Krilich's Kangaroos ran riot at a packed Hull City football ground, nobody was left in any doubt. Things were summed up in one specific moment in the 1982 second Test at Wigan when Wally Lewis hit Meninga on the chest with a 25-yard bullet pass to send big Mal over for a try, and the Central Park crowd just gasped in awe.

1983 - Lang Park, Brisbane - Australia 12, New Zealand 19.
A pivotal moment in the rise of Rugby League in New Zealand as the Kiwis beat the supposedly 'unbeatable' Aussies on their own turf under the Lang Park floodlights. It marked the arrival of new coach Graham Lowe, as the Kiwis captained by Graeme West took Australia apart - first with rugged defence by Kurt Sorensen and Mark Broadhurst, and then sparkling attack by the likes of Fred Ah Kuoi, James Leuluai, Shane Varley and Joe Ropati.

1985 - Carlaw Park, Auckland - New Zealand 18, Australia 0.
This stunning victory for the Kiwis in the first qualifying game in the new World Cup format has to be put into the context of what had gone before just a week earlier at Carlaw Park. Then, New Zealand had reached new heights of performance in a magnificent Test match, only to be denied a deserved victory by a controversial breakaway try by Australia in the dying seconds. Emotionally shattered, the Kiwis vowed to come back and they did ... with a bang, to wallop an Aussie side controversially changed by coach Terry Fearnley. This game saw Mark Graham, fully fit for once, at his brilliant best as scrum-half Clayton Friend scored two tries, to seal a series which had a nationwide audience in New Zealand glued to their t.v. sets as Rugby League in their country won the widespread acclaim it had never known before.

1985 - Headingley, Leeds - Great Britain 22, New Zealand 24.
Great Britain lost this Test, but Rugby League truly was the winner as a new era for Test football dawned. In perfect conditions, both sides served up an attacking feast, as the British saw a new generation of young back-line stars like Hanley, Lydon, Schofield, Myler and Fox confirm their potential. This game included one of the great Test match tries, scored by Joe Lydon after Ellery Hanley had sprinted along the grandstand side at Headingley and thrown the ball inside. It was just the opening salvo in a Test series which won a new audience for the international game and enabled Great Britain to emerge from the dark days of defeat in had been enduring. Much drama followed, both in the second Test when Garry Schofield scored four tries in a stunning British victory, and the third when brawling and mayhem was followed by a series-levelling last minute penalty goal by Lee Crooks.

1986 - Old Trafford, Manchester - Great Britain 16, Australia 38.
It was an incredible feeling to be at Old Trafford, in the pouring rain, and see a crowd of 50,583 attend this first Test. The Aussies were back for the first time since the 'Invincibles' tour of 1982, and British coach Maurice Bamford had successfully built up the public's hopes that his Great Britain side could match them. On the field, it proved to be another masterclass from a new team in the green and gold, but attracting a crowd like that was just sensational.

1988 - Sydney Football Stadium - Australia 12, Great Britain 26.
A wonderful moment of relief for Great Britain as their patched-up and injury-hit side shocked Australia with this epic victory. It was Britain's first Test win over the Aussies for ten years, and a major triumph for coach Malcolm Reilly and captain Ellery Hanley. Still the memories are clear of the British tries: Phil Ford 'he's a stepper'; Henderson Gill 'does a bit of a boogie'; and the clinching magnificent sight of Mike Gregory striding out to score.

(Above, left)
Australian captain Wally Lewis leads his team against New Zealand at Carlaw Park in the truly epic 1985 Test series between the two Anzac nations. Garry Jack and Mal Meninga are in support of their skipper as the Kiwi hooker Howie Tamati watches closely.

(Above, right)
Great Britain full-back Joe Lydon sprints down the touchline at Old Trafford in the first Test versus Australia in 1986, on the way to one of the best tries ever seen in Ashes history. Winger Henderson Gill is in support, but Lydon did not need him as he out-paced the Australian full-back Garry Jack to slide over and score in the corner. The previous year, against New Zealand in the first Test at Headingley, Lydon has scored an equally memorable longe-range try - this time as a winger.

RUGBY LEAGUE SUPERSTARS

(Right)
Three of British Rugby League's brightest stars of the 'eighties - Ellery Hanley, Des Drummond, and Henderson Gill - on Test match duty in France in 1986 and getting to grips with a new fangled invention called a 'walkman'.

(Below)
Joe Lydon and Andy Gregory celebrate a Wembley win with Widnes in 1984 - both would return to their home town Wigan to continue as two of the decade's biggest stars.

British Rugby League enjoyed a new generation of star players, most of whom came to prominence after the watershed of the 1982 Ashes defeat. In the compilation of this book, we constantly came across photos of the likes of Garry Schofield, Ellery Hanley, Joe Lydon and Henderson Gill, so often did they crop up as key players for both club and country. Add to them such names as Des Drummond, Andy Gregory, Shaun Edwards and Tony Myler, and you can see just how blessed the British game was with backline stars. And then, in 1987, came a new boy called Martin Offiah who, after just one season in the game with Widnes, had won the 'Man of Steel' award, finished top try-scorer and become a Lions tourist. Of course, no name and no presence was bigger than Ellery Hanley, who became 'Man of Steel' three times and starred on two Lions tours in the 'eighties.

MEN OF STEEL

1980 - George Fairbairn *(Wigan)*
1981 - Ken Kelly *(Warrington)*
1982 - Mick Morgan *(Carlisle)*
1983 - Allan Agar *(Featherstone)*
1984 - Joe Lydon *(Widnes)*
1985 - Ellery Hanley *(Bradford)*
1986 - Gavin Miller *(Hull K.R.)*
1987 - Ellery Hanley *(Wigan)*
1988 - Martin Offiah *(Widnes)*
1989 - Ellery Hanley *(Wigan)*

(Above) The Iro brothers, Tony *(left)* and Kevin, arrived at Wigan from New Zealand in the late 1980s and immediately became two new stars.

LIFE IN THE SECOND DIVISION

(Left) Tony Rose, in action for Whitehaven versus Rochdale Hornets. The Leeds based Rose was a popular forward for the Cumbrians, and also played for Huddersfield and Dewsbury in the '80s.

(Below) John Buckton playing for Doncaster against Rochdale, was a prolific try-scorer for the Dons in the 1980s.

(Below) Marching orders for Workington Town forward Ian Hartley from referee David Croft at Halifax in September 1984.

(Above) Nigel Stephenson in action for Huddersfield in the 1988-89 season - Nigel had a wonderful professional career stretching over 20 years.

(Far right) Carl Gibson attacks for Batley in 1983-84 - he was picked for Great Britain in 1985 and soon after signed by Leeds for £50,000.

Timeline
1980

(Above)
Harry Beverley - was signed by Fulham on the eve of their debut match against Wigan in September 1980, and became one of the giant pack who were such favourites at Craven Cottage.

Rugby League received a massive boost in the first year of 1980s with the launch of the Fulham team, the first professional club in London for over 40 years. Fulham's impact on the game was immense, not least because they injected considerable new funds into the transfer market, then kicked off by attracting a 9,554 crowd to a Second Division match and went on to achieve a season's league average of 6,096 – making them the fourth best supported club in the country, behind only the Humberside giants of Hull and Hull K.R. and (very marginally) the First Division champions Bradford Northern. Fulham also showed the potential for big-time Rugby League in the capital city when they drew significant crowds to first round knockout Cup matches at Craven Cottage: 12,583 against Leeds in the John Player Trophy and 15,013 versus Wakefield Trinity in the Challenge Cup.

Before Fulham's arrival began dominating the headlines, much of Rugby League's focus was on the city of Hull, where both clubs continued to grow at pace. Hull F.C., in particular, had made rapid strides since winning promotion back to the First Division in 1978-79, spending big money to recruit players, culminating when they set a new Rugby League transfer fee record of £40,000 in 1980 to sign Trevor Skerrett from Wakefield. The 'Airlie Birds' were the game's top supported club and their city was brought to a standstill on 3rd May 1980 when Hull and Hull K.R. met in the Challenge Cup Final at Wembley. It was Rovers who prevailed, winning 10-5 in front of a capacity crowd of 95,000 and their captain Roger Millward, at last at Wembley for the first time after such a long and illustrious career, received the Cup from the Queen Mother. Millward had played on bravely in that Cup Final despite having his jaw broken, and in October of 1980 Roger finally called it quits and hung up his boots after suffering his fourth broken jaw in 12 months in an 'A' team match against Batley.

The 'unthinkable' happened in 1980 as Wigan were relegated to the Second Division. They appointed full-back George Fairbairn as player-coach for the 1980-81 season, with the almost mandatory requirement of winning promotion. Fairbairn, a Scotsman who qualified for England under the grandparent ruling, had been involved in one of the most controversial international matches seen for many years when England beat France 4-2 in Narbonne on 16th March 1980 to claim the European Championship. In a white hot atmosphere, a French crowd estimated at anything between 15,000 and 20,000 bayed for the blood of English referee Billy Thompson after he had incensed them with his decisions. The English were even more incensed by outbreaks of blatant brutality from some of the French players which led to RFL council member Bill Oxley calling for matches against France to be stopped 'until they get their house in order'.

The world of sport in 1980

* A total of 65 Olympic member countries boycott the Moscow games, chiefly because of the American protest at Russia's invasion of Afghanistan.
* At those Moscow Olympics, British athletes Steve Ovett and Sebastian Coe win a gold medal each.
* Nottingham Forest, managed by Brian Clough, win the European Cup for the second year in a row.
* Welsh forward Paul Ringer becomes the first man to be sent off in a Rugby Union international at Twickenham since 1925.
* Severiano Ballesteros becomes the first European golfer to win the the U.S. Masters at Augusta.
* Captained by Lancastrian Bill Beaumont, the British Lions Rugby Union team tour apartheid-ridden South Africa, losing 3-1 to the Springboks.

The international game enjoyed much happier moments later in 1980 when a New Zealand touring team visited England and won many friends with their attractive style of play - the Kiwis achieving a drawn Test series against Great Britain, for whom Johnny Whiteley had been reinstated as coach (having been the man at the helm when Britain last won the Ashes in 1970).

Things were changing in the television coverage of Rugby League in 1980 as ITV, via their northern regional stations Granada and Yorkshire Television, finally broke the long held monopoly of the BBC. The 'Beeb' agreed a new contract with the RFL which would see them broadcasting only Cup games and knock-out competitions plus internationals, leaving the ITV regions to cover any league games. In addition, the BBC announced they were dropping the very popular Floodlit Trophy after suggesting that most club's floodlights were not good enough for colour television and it had been costing the BBC themselves £9,000 per match to provide suitable lighting. Leeds became the last club to switch their regular home games to Sundays in the 1980-81 season, and sponsorship continued to make inroads as Websters brewery added their backing to the Yorkshire Cup and Featherstone Rovers became the first club to carry the name of a commercial sponsor across their jerseys when local company Linpac agreed a £10,000 deal.

(Above) **Roger Millward holds the Challenge Cup aloft on the shoulders of his Hull Kingston Rovers colleagues after their victory over neighbours Hull in the 1980 Final at Wembley.**

(Above, left) **Steve Quinn wearing the Linpac logo as Featherstone led the way in advertising a sponsor on their jersey. Quinn was the game's top goal-kicker in 1979-80.**
(Above, right) **Trevor Skerrett was the game's most expensive player when Hull paid a record transfer fee of £40,000 to sign him in 1980.**

TOP TEN

1979-80
TRIES
30 **Keith Fielding** (Salford)
30 **Steve Hubbard** (Hull K.R.)
29 **Geoff Munro** (Oldham)
27 **Ian Ball** (Barrow)
27 **Keith Bentley** (Widnes)
27 **Peter Glynn** (St.Helens)
27 **Roy Mathias** (St.Helens)
26 **John Bevan** (Warrington)
26 **David Redfearn** (Bradford)
24 **David Smith** (Leeds)

GOALS
163 **Steve Quinn** (Featherstone)
138 **Steve Hubbard** (Hull K.R.)
134 **Steve Rule** (Salford)
128 **Steve Hesford** (Warrington)
127 **Mick Burke** (Widnes)
119 **Ian Ball** (Barrow)
116 **Steve Diamond** (Wakefield)
108 **Eric Fitzsimons** (Oldham)
 98 **Mick Parrish** (Hunslet)
 97 **Jimmy Birts** (Halifax)

Timeline
1981

In the 1980-81 season Bradford Northern became the first team to win the Championship in successive seasons since the reintroduction of two divisions in 1973, and thus they emulated the achievement of Swinton who had performed a similar double in 1962-63 and 1963-64. Sponsorship had arrived for the first time in the Championship, with winners Bradford being awarded prize money of £6,000 as part of a three-year package from Slalom Lager worth a total of £215,000 to the game. Coached by Peter Fox, Northern retained the title in 1981 after a close battle with runners-up Warrington, who became victims of a hectic schedule in which they played nine games in 23 days to make up a backlog caused by their success in the various cup competitions.

Not long after lifting the Championship trophy at Odsal, the vastly experienced Jimmy Thompson and Nigel Stephenson, along with a third Bradford Northern player Steve Ferres, were on their way to Carlisle to become foundation players of the new club which entered in the league in 1981-82. Carlisle, along with the Welsh side Cardiff City, were the two football teams - from a long reported list of potential applicants - who emerged as the serious candidates to follow in the very successful footsteps of Fulham. The Londoners had won promotion at the first attempt in 1981, and attracted big crowds and joyous times to Craven Cottage, and the game's geographical spread was further increased from south Wales to the Scottish border with the arrival of Cardiff and Carlisle. The 'Blue Dragons' kicked off in similar style to Fulham, in a blaze of publicity and with a near 10,000 crowd for their opening match versus Salford at Ninian Park, but it was the more modest Carlisle who came through most successfully on the field, under coach Allan Agar, to win promotion in their first season.

No sooner had George Fairbairn led Wigan to promotion in 1981 than he was sacked from the coaching job, Wigan believing he lacked the experience to coach in the first division. Wigan, eventually, appointed the Yorkshireman Maurice Bamford and faced a struggle to hold on to the disappointed Fairbairn as a player. George had captained both Great Britain and England during the 1980-81 season and in the summer of 1981 he became the game's most expensive player when Hull K.R. smashed the world transfer record to get him, setting the bar at a new high of £72,500. Big money transfer deals, or potential deals, made constant headlines in 1981, with the presence of the three new clubs - Fulham, Cardiff and Carlisle - inflating the market. And another club recruiting heavily was Blackpool Borough who, with investment from a new chairman, rebranded themselves as 'The

(Above)
Jimmy Thompson and Nigel Stephenson lift the Championship trophy for Bradford Northern in 1981 - later that year they both joined the new Carlisle club.

The world of sport in 1981

* Liverpool become the first British team to win the European Cup three times - a goal by Alan Kennedy brings a Final victory over Real Madrid.
* In an incredible cricket comeback at Headingley, Ian Botham's brilliance with both bat and ball inspires a sensational Test win over Australia.
* Anti-apartheid protest battles surround the Springboks tour to New Zealand, as Rugby Union brings violent unrest and shame to the country.
* Bob Champion and horse Aldaniti create great emotion as they win the Grand National.
* The first London Marathon is staged with 7.055 runners entering the race.
* Ipswich Town with the UEFA Cup.
* Bill Shankly dies in a Liverpool hospital aged 67.

Milers' and abandoned their iconic tangerine, black and white colours in favour of new kit in green and largely black. It didn't last long. Meanwhile recruitment was extending overseas again, and with the transfer ban still preventing clubs signing players from Australia, all eyes turned to the New Zealanders who had made such a good impression on their 1980 tour. Hull hit the jackpot by signing Gary Kemble, James Leuluai and Dane O'Hara, and the trio played together for the first time at the Boulevard on September 28th 1981, as a 16,157 crowd turned out to welcome them. Meanwhile, the Kiwi scrum-half Shane Varley was signed by Workington Town and forward Ray Baxendale by Wakefield Trinity.

(*Above*) John Crossley, the York stand-off, pictured scoring one of the 35 touchdowns which made him the game's top try-scorer in 1980-81. Soon after, he was signed by the big-spending Fulham club.

(*Above*) Blackpool Boro's attractive big-format programme as they tried to create a new image as 'The Milers' in 1981. (*Right*) The controversial referee Guy Cattaneo at Headingley for the England-France game in 1981.

The influence of sponsorship continued to grow and the Challenge Cup Final was rebranded from State Express to be under the banner of 'Three Fives' in 1981 - on the field it made little difference as Widnes continued their Wembley successes of the previous decade. On the international front, there was more controversy over a referee in an England-France game, this time it was the French official Guy Cattaneo who was castigated for his unashamedly biased display as France beat England 5-1 at Headingley in February 1981. The French had already beaten Wales convincingly so they took the rather hollow crown of European Champions as they prepared for their first major tour down-under since 1964. Alas, even worse drama hit the game in France when their 1981 Championship Final was abandoned after four minutes of mayhem in Toulouse. For the British game, such a disappointing loss to France by England, following the unimpressive Test displays against the 1980 Kiwis, left many question marks for the international management team of Johnny Whiteley and Colin Hutton as they looked ahead to the 1982 Ashes. A return to full Great Britain-France Test matches came in December 1981, with each country winning well on their home soil. On a happier note, the first Varsity match was played between Oxford and Cambridge Universities in 1981.

TOP TEN

1980-81

TRIES

35	John Crossley	(York)
28	Terry Richardson	(Castleford)
25	Steve Hubbard	(Hull K.R.)
23	Steve Hartley	(Hull K.R.)
23	Paul McDermott	(York)
23	Ian Slater	(Huddersfield)
20	Des Drummond	(Leigh)
19	Ian Ball	(Barrow)
19	John Bevan	(Warrington)
19	Peter Cramp	(Huddersfield)
19	Gary Hyde	(Castleford)
19	Dennis Ramsdale	(Wigan)

GOALS

147	Steve Hesford	(Warrington)
123	Steve Quinn	(Featherstone)
112	Steve Diamond	(Wakefield)
110	Mick Burke	(Widnes)
109	Steve Hubbard	(Hull K.R.)
104	Ian Ball	(Barrow)
100	Jimmy Birts	(Halifax)
97	Graham Beale	(Keighley)
93	Mick Parrish	(Oldham)
94	George Fairbairn	(Wigan)

Timeline
1982

Everything that happened in Rugby League in 1982 paled into insignificance when set alongside the impact made by the Australian touring team which swept through both Britain and France unbeaten. The 1982 Kangaroos not only retained the Ashes with a first ever three Tests to nil whitewash on British soil, they redefined the way Rugby League could be played. That meant, forever after, the rest of the world would look to Australia for guidance when it came to coaching and player preparation.

Before the first Test of the 1982 Ashes series at Boothferry Park in Hull, British Rugby League was happily getting on with its own business and feeling pretty positive about things. Great optimism had been generated by the replay of the Challenge Cup Final between Hull and Widnes, which became necessary after the teams had drawn 14-all at Wembley. It was the first time since 1954 that the Rugby League had to arrange a Cup Final replay - and, just as back on that famous night at Odsal stadium 28 years earlier - the game confirmed its enormous strength on home soil in the north of England as a somewhat unexpected wave of support packed Elland Road to its rafters and produced a white-hot atmosphere for what turned out to be an epic event. The replayed final saw Hull, captained by the former Wakefield skipper David Topliss, win the Cup for the first time in 68 years in front of a capacity crowd of over 41,000 - the biggest attendance for a game in England outside of Wembley since the 1962 Cup semi-final between Wakefield and Featherstone at Odsal. The successful Hull club further contributed to the 'feelgood factor' by increasing attendance figures again to be the game's best supported team in 1981-82 season with an average crowd of 13,190 for their league fixtures at the Boulevard. Overall, first division total crowd figures reached a new record level since two divisions were introduced in 1973.

(Above)
Steve Donlan - a key man for Leigh as they won the Championship in 1982. Donlan played 41 games in their successful campaign.

The world of sport in 1982

* The football World Cup is staged in Spain with Italy the winners. Their hero is Paolo Rossi as they beat West Germany 3-1 in the final.
* Daley Thompson wins the decathlon gold medal at the European Athletics championships in Athens, setting a new world record in the process.
* The Middlesex and England spin bowler Fred Titmus retires after a 33-year cricket career.
* Aston Villa become the fourth English club to win the European Cup, as they beat Bayern Munich in the final 1-0 with a Peter Withe goal.
* American Tom Watson becomes the fifth golfer to win the Open and US Open in the same year.
* Jimmy Connors wins the Wimbledon men's title.

There was no little drama as Leigh were crowned Champions in 1982 - their first title for 76 years. The destiny of the Championship came down to the last 40 minutes of Leigh's season and was fought out at the unlikely setting of Whitehaven's Recreation Ground. Needing only a draw to clinch the title, Leigh travelled for a midweek game at Whitehaven accompanied by around 4,000 fans. Trailing 4-1 to the first division's bottom team at half-time, Leigh rallied to win 13-4 in the second half and, amid delirous scenes in Cumbria, their captain John Woods was carried shoulder-high to receive the trophy. In the Second Division, Oldham were champions and the new club Carlisle achieved promotion, with Mick Morgan winning the coveted 'Man of Steel'

Hull win the Cup

(Above) **Hull F.C. finally got their hands on the Challenge Cup again in 1982 - but not at Wembley - as their captain David Topliss lifts the trophy after the thrilling replay win over Widnes at Elland Road, Leeds.**

award after setting a new record for a prop forward of 25 tries. Other notable landmarks included an MBE in the 1982 New Year's honours list for Eddie Waring, in the year after he retired as BBC's 'voice of Rugby League' following 30 years at the t.v. microphone. And at Salford, the Snape family's long and successful control of the club was ended when a local businessman, John Wilkinson, was appointed Chairman.

As the underlying dispute between BARLA and the RFL over youth teams continued to simmer, the professionals undertook their first Colts tour to Australia, with Hull's Lee Crooks captaining the British side. Teenager Crooks had a memorable 1982, playing in Hull's Challenge Cup winning team and making his full Test debut againt Australia. Following the impact made by the Kangaroo tourists it was a major surprise in late 1982 when the International Board voted to maintain the Anglo-Australia transfers ban. Rugby League returned to Italy in July of 1982 when Great Britain and France played in an exhibition match in Venice, and a step forward for the British game was made when Phil Larder became full-time National Coaching director in 1982.

(Above) **Carlisle began their second season in 1982 with three signings from New Zealand: Dean Bell, Ian Bell and Clayton Friend. Dean Bell played for Cumbria, on residency grounds, against the 1982 Kangaroos.**

TOP TEN

1981-82

TRIES

31	**Johnny Jones** (Workington)
26	**Des Drummond** (Leigh)
26	**John Basnett** (Widnes)
26	**Ray Ashton** (Oldham)
25	**Mick Morgan** (Carlisle)
23	**Steve Hartley** (Hull K.R.)
23	**Lynn Hopkins** (Workington)
23	**Terry Day** (Hull)
22	**Steve Evans** (Featherstn.&Hull)
21	**David Hobbs** (Featherstone)
21	**David Moll** (Keighley)

GOALS

190	**Lynn Hopkins** (Workington)
168	**George Fairbairn** (Wigan)
164	**Mick Parrish** (Oldham)
158	**John Woods** (Leigh)
130	**Steve Rule** (Salford)
125	**Kevin Dick** (Leeds)
120	**Steve Quinn** (Featherstone)
119	**Malcolm Agar** (Halifax)
118	**Lee Crooks** (Hull)
116	**Steve Hesford** (Warrington)

Timeline
1983

In the initial aftermath of the 1982 'Invincibles' Kangaroos tour, British Rugby League spent the early months of 1983 feeling rather shell-shocked - but the game soon emerged to enjoy a remarkably busy and eventful year. The Great Britain team took their first steps in trying rebuild a shattered reputation by beating France home and away in early 1983, but both Tests were scrappy, niggling affairs which did little to enhance the image of the game. With the Hull K.R. tough guy Len Casey as captain, and a new coach in Frank Myler replacing Johnny Whiteley, the British team management endured a war of words with the referee, New Zealander Don Wilson, who was not impressed by what he had seen. The quality of those European Tests was in stark contrast to the contest seen in Brisbane later in the year when New Zealand won a remarkable victory over the supposedly 'unbeatable' Australians.

(Above)
Queensland forward Greg Dowling tests the Wigan defence as the tourists cantered to a 40-2 win at Central Park in 1983. Dowling would return to play for Wigan two years later.

A bright spot in Great Britain's 17-5 win over France in a brawling affair at the Boulevard was a classic try by the French winger Patrick Solal, which prompted the ambitious Hull club to sign him. Solal thus became the first Frenchman to play at the top level with an English club, and he was a part of the Hull squad which clinched the Championship title in 1983. The 'Airlie Birds' were unable to make that a 'double' with the Challenge Cup as they were beaten by underdogs Featherstone in an emotional and nail-biting Wembley final.

Some very significant decisions were taken by the game's ruling bodies which were to prove very influential on the game's rise as the decade progressed. In addition to the introduction of the four-point try and the sin-bin, a new season kicked off in August 1983 with a major new rule in place which saw a scrum after the sixth tackle replaced by a handover of possession - this was to prove hugely important in shaping the modern game, with fewer scrums and much greater importance placed on a variety of tactical kicking. In addition, the rule was changed so that the non-offending team had both head and feed at a scrum. Another key decision taken by the Rugby League Council was the lifting of the ban on transfers between Britain and Australia - which initially saw a trickle of Aussies coming to

The world of sport in 1983

* Aberdeen, managed by up and coming Alex Ferguson, with the European Cup Winners' Cup, beating Real Madrid in the final in Gothenburg.
* Newcastle Polytechnic student Steve Cram wins gold in the 1,500 metres at the athletics world championships staged in Helsinki.
* Australia wins the America's Cup in yachting, in a campaign headed by Perth millionaire Alan Bond.
* In Rugby Union, the British Lions have a dismal tour of New Zealand, losing all four Tests.
* The champion race-horse Shergar goes missing in Ireland, the £10 million pound stallion is kidnapped and a £2 million ransom demanded.
* Brighton and Hove Albion reach the F.A.Cup Final and draw 2-2 with Manchester United at Wembley.

1983 was a year when the underdogs had their day in Rugby League in spectacular style. Barrow won the Lancashire Cup, and *(above, left)* their captain Alan Hodkinson is pictured in action in the Final in which they beat the so called 'cup kings' of Widnes, 12-8, at Central Park. Meanwhile, at Wembley, Featherstone Rovers with a team of home grown local lads, beat the hot favourites Hull to win the Challenge Cup for the third time in their history. *(Above, right)* Lance Todd Trophy winner David Hobbs - scorer of both his team's tries - celebrates with winger John Marsden moments after the final whistle blew. Featherstone were coached by the former Carlisle boss Allan Agar, who was named the 'Man of Steel' for 1983

England, notably the Queenslander Terry Webb and former Manly scrum-half Steve Martin to Leeds - but would eventually lead to several stars of the 1982 Kangaroo team returning to brighten up the English scene. The autumn of 1983 was already lit up by the visit of two first time touring teams to England - the Queensland State team, captained by Wally Lewis, and the New Zealand Maori team, whose tour was hosted to by BARLA.

The British game already was seeing a new breed of young players beginning to emerge, and this rich crop of talent was perfectly illustrated by the BARLA Young Lions touring team which travelled to New Zealand in the summer of 1983. Many of them returned to be successful with professional clubs, with some like: Garry Schofield, David Creasser, Gary Divorty, Mike Ford and Deryck Fox, going on to instant fame and full Test honours. Schofield won his first Test cap after just 16 first team games as a professional, and Fox was elected by the R.L. Players' Association as their player-of-the-year at the end of his first season with Featherstone Rovers. With other young stars like Joe Lydon, Tony Myler and Andy Gregory emerging, the future for the British game looked brighter already. And Wigan made the most high profile junior signing of all time when schoolboy star Shaun Edwards agreed a contract reported to be worth £35,000 just seconds after midnight on 17th October 1983 as he turned 17. The signing was shown nationwide on BBC television's 'Breakfast Time' programme a few hours later. That came after earlier national publicity had heralded the arrival of yet another new club, Kent Invicta, based at Maidstone, who became the southern most professional club in the game's history.

TOP TEN

1982-83

TRIES

37	**Bob Eccles** (Warrington)
28	**Steve Evans** (Hull)
27	**John Crossley** (Fulham)
26	**Tommy David** (Cardiff City)
24	**David Topliss** (Hull)
23	**Hussein M'Barki** (Fulham)
22	**Gary Hyde** (Castleford)
22	**Paul McDermott** (York)
21	**James Leuluai** (Hull)
20	**Phil Ford** (Warrington)
20	**Garry Clark** (Hull K.R.)

GOALS

136	**Steve Diamond** (Fulham)
121	**Eric Fitzsimons** (Hunslet)
120	**Lee Crooks** (Hull)
117	**Bob Beardmore** (Castleford)
113	**Steve Hesford** (Warrington)
111	**Steve Fenwick** (Cardiff City)
110	**Ken Jones** (Swinton)
104	**Colin Whitfield** (Wigan)
104	**Shaun Kilner** (Bramley)
98	**Steve Quinn** (Featherstone)

Timeline
1984

In a year when some of Australia's biggest stars began to provide a major boost to the English club game, none could outshine the impact made by a new young British star, Ellery Hanley. The Bradford Northern stand-off began to make his mark in the international arena after making his Test debut as a substitute against France at Avignon on 29th January 1984. Hanley was one of several exciting young players to return from the 1984 Lions tour with their reputations enhanced, despite Great Britain losing all six Tests in Australia and New Zealand for the first time. Hanley's potential had long been championed by 'Open Rugby' magazine and it was fitting that Ellery was the recipient of their prestigious medal award in 1984 for his peformances on the tour and overall influence on the game.

The first big names from the 1982 Kangaroo touring team arrived to play for English clubs just before the end of 1983 - and their impact was immediate as a crowd over three times Wakefield Trinity's usual home attendance turned out to see Wally Lewis make his debut facing Peter Sterling (playing for Hull). It was a massive coup for Wakefield, struggling against relegation, to get Wally Lewis, on a reported £1,000 a game paid for by sponsor Barry Hough. Lewis played just 10 games for Wakefield, with a mere four at Belle Vue, yet his impact on the club remains part of Trinity's folklore. Wally returned home after his spell with Wakefield to captain Australia as they retained the Ashes against a Lions team skippered by Brian Noble. In the autumn of 1984 both Peter Sterling at Hull and Mal Meninga at St.Helens helped make the County Cup Finals the best supported for many years - and before the year was out Wigan welcomed another two Aussies, winger John Ferguson and 1982 tourist Brett Kenny, who would go on to shine so brightly in the months that followed.

(Above)
Mick Adams sets up the play for Widnes in their 1984 Cup semi-final win over Leeds. Adams went on to be vice-captain of the 1984 Lions.

Whilst the top level of the game was enjoying all this excitement, things were not looking so good lower down the divisions as the new clubs, which had started with such optimism, now found themselves in battles for survival. Fulham had been jetisoned by the football club at Craven Cottage and were saved by Roy Close, a Maidenhead businessman, and his wife Barbara (who became Rugby League's first ever female chairperson). After weeks of uncertainty, they found a new home ground for their club at the Crystal Palace athletics stadium, but were left to rebuild a team after a controversial legal judgement made the Fulham players free agents. Erstwhile leader Reg Bowden joined Warrington,

The world of sport in 1984

* In the Los Angeles Olympic Games, Daley Thompson wins his second decathlon gold medal.
* Other British winners include javelin thrower Tessa Sanderson, based at Carnegie College, Leeds.
* Watford, backed by singer Elton John, reach the F.A.Cup Final, but are beaten 2-0 by Everton.
* Controversy at the Olympics as South African girl Zola Budd, running for Britain, is involved in a clash which decks America's darling Mary Decker.
* France win the European Football Championship, on home soil, inspired by Michel Platini.
* John McEnroe destroys Jimmy Connors in three easy sets to win the Wimbledon men's tennis title.
* Niki Lauda, back after being badly burnt in a 1976 crash, wins the world drivers' championship.

along with several other of Fulham's favourites and Roy Lester - who had been the first player to sign for Fulham in 1980 - took over as manager-coach. It was a similar story for Cardiff as their parent football club had enough of Rugby League and the Blue Dragons had to leave Ninian Park, moving to Bridgend. Meanwhile, after just one season at Maidstone Football Club, Kent Invicta were placed under new management and moved to Southend. Despite all these struggles, it did not stop yet more people wanting to start clubs and in 1984 both Sheffield Eagles and Mansfield Marksman were accepted into the Rugby League. There was also another new name, rather embarrasingly, as Huddersfield started calling themselves the Barracudas, and renamed Fartown as 'Arena '84'.

This was the year when the Alliance League was founded in an attempt to reinvigorate reserve team rugby as the long established Lancashire Combination and Yorkshire Senior Competition were abandoned. Great Britain got a new coach when Frank Myler stood down after the 1984 Lions tour, and was replaced by Maurice Bamford. The new coach's first chance to organise an international side came with an Under-21 match in November, won by his British boys 24-8 over France at Castleford. Another well known coach, Alex Murphy, had replaced Bamford at Wigan and found himself back at Wembley for the 1984 Cup Final - Wigan flew Australian prop Kerry Hemsley back to play in the Final but it was all to no avail as they were well beaten by Widnes. Ironically, it was a Wigan lad, Joe Lydon, who did most to beat them with two long range tries which helped him with the Lance Todd Trophy. Just two years earlier Lydon had played for his school in the very first 'Open Rugby' Cup Final, and it was a sign of the remarkable progress made by the British Upper Schools & Colleges R.L. Association that they were able to undertake a tour to Australia in 1984.

(Above) **Joe Lydon heads for one of his brace of spectacular tries for Widnes at Wembley against Wigan in the 1984 Cup Final, and also on his way to the Lance Todd trophy.**

TOP TEN

1983-84

TRIES

38	**Garry Schofield** (Hull)
28	**Joe Lydon** (Widnes)
28	**Graham King** (Hunslet)
27	**John Woods** (Leigh)
26	**John Basnett** (Widnes)
26	**Carl Gibson** (Batley)
25	**Steve Herbert** (Barrow)
25	**Graham Steadman** (York)
25	**Gary Prohm** (Hull K.R.)
24	**Garry Clark** (Hull K.R.)

GOALS

142	**Steve Hesford** (Warrington)
142	**Bob Beardmore** (Castleford)
140	**Lynn Hallett** (Cardiff City)
131	**Eric Fitzsimons** (Hunslet)
124	**John Woods** (Leigh)
122	**Colin Whitfield** (Wigan)
104	**Ian Ball** (Barrow)
101	**Mick Parrish** (Oldham)
94	**Malcolm Agar** (Halifax)
91	**Steve Tickle** (Barrow)

Timeline
1985

(Right)
Ellery Hanley - the player whose star quality dominated Rugby League in 1985, pictured diving over to score for Bradford Northern. Playing almost exclusively at stand-off in the 1984-85 season, Ellery scored an incredible 55 tries (made up of 52 for his club Bradford, two for Great Britain and one for England) from a total of 40 games. This achievement meant he became the first player to score over 50 tries in a season since Billy Boston did it back in 1961-62. Hanley 's 55 tries were the most ever by a non-winger and he also set a new record of 40 Division One tries

In the modern history of Rugby League, in picking a 'glory year' it would be hard to find anything to better 1985. Both in the domestic game in Britain and on the international front, Rugby League began to hit new heights. For the British game so much progress had been made since the rude awakening of the 1982 Kangaroo tour, and a new optimism was being promoted. The jewel in the game's crown was the 1985 Challenge Cup Final in which Wigan and Hull produced a high-scoring classic to celebrate the 50th Wembley final, and provided an epic sporting occasion which won the admiration of the nation. Overseas players played a big part in that Final, with much of the focus on the half-backs from the 1982 Kangaroos and the successful Parramatta club in Sydney - Brett Kenny and Peter Sterling - playing against each other. They both lived up to expectations, but it was the brilliance of Brett Kenny, along with Wigan's Australian winger John Ferguson, which came out on top. Kenny became the first Australian to win the Lance Todd Trophy and Wigan skipper Graeme West the first New Zealand captain to lift the Cup since Ces Mountford in 1951. Young British stars like Shaun Edwards, Mike Ford and Henderson Gill also shone brightly at Wembley on a glorious day for the game. Due to public demand, Wembley's capacity was extended past the recent limit of 95,000, and it was a sign of the great decade which followed that Wigan, the game's most celebrated club, finally got their hands on the Cup again after a gap of 20 years.

The world of sport in 1985

* Tragedy strikes at Bradford City's Valley Parade on 11th May as a fire in the grandstand leaves 40 people dead and many more seriously injured.
* Less than three weeks after the Bradford fire, more tragedy for football as 41 Juventus fans are killed before the European Cup final against Liverpool at the Heysel Stadium in Brussels.
* Jock Stein, the man who guided Glasgow Celtic to glory, dies - aged 62 - at Cardiff's Ninian Park.
* Dennis Taylor wins snooker's world championship, watched by 18.5 million t.v. viewers.
* Another Ulsterman, boxer Barry McGuigan, becomes a world champion featherweight.
*Everton win the European Cup Winners' Cup.
* Boris Becker, aged 17, becomes Wimbledon's youngest ever, and first unseeded, champion.

Not to be outdone by their local rivals, St.Helens followed that great Wembley final with some glory of their own seven days later by winning the Premiership Final against Hull K.R., inspired by the Saints' own Aussie hero, Mal Meninga. The St.Helens captain that day was Harry Pinner, and the skillful loose-forward was chosen by coach Maurice Bamford to lead the Great Britain team when the Kiwis arrived later in 1985 for the most eagerly anticipated visit of any New Zealand team. The Kiwis had just taken part in a truly epic series against Australia, which finished with a stunning 18-nil win for Graham Lowe's team, and the three Tests in England enabled the game to continue where it had left off at the 1985 Wembley final - at last with full coverage of every Test on live television by the BBC, nationwide viewers enjoyed two wonderful exhibitions of open, attacking play in glorious autumn sunshine as the Kiwis edged home narrowly in the first Test at Headingley, followed by a stunning revenge by Great Britain at Wigan in which young centre Garry Schofield wrote himself into the record books with four glorious tries. The deciding third Test at Elland Road turned into a war of attrition, rough and tough, with spectators on the edge of their seats as Lee Crooks stepped up to kick a last minute equalising penalty goal which produced a drawn series.

Ellery Hanley was the name everybody was talking about, as he starred for Great Britain and became the first man to score more than 50 tries in a season for 23 years. In September 1985 Hanley left Bradford Northern to join Wigan in a record transfer deal worth £150,000 (£85,000 cash plus internationals Phil Ford and Steve Donlan). Such commercial vibrancy in the game was further illustrated by Whitbread's sponsorship of the Great Britain team and the Test series and the creation of new sponsored competitions, the Rodstock 'War of the Roses' and the Charity Shield staged on the Isle of Man. In addition the Golden Boot award was launched by *Open Rugby* with the first winner Wally Lewis being presented with it in Brisbane. Not so positive was the withdrawal of both Bridgend and Southend from the league before the 1985-86 season; and sadly in 1985 the game mourned the deaths of two of the great figures in its history: Clive Sullivan, World Cup winning captain, and Bill Fallowfield, former RFL secretary and International Board pioneer.

(Pictured above) **Just two of the magical moments of 1985 as** *(left)* **Henderson Gill dives ahead of the Hull winger Kevin James in the Cup Final at Wembley in which Gill scored a wonderful try; and** *(right)* **centre Garry Schofield is congratulated by Ellery Hanley as he scored four tries for Great Britain in the stunning 25-8 Second Test win over New Zealand.**

TOP TEN

1984-85

TRIES

55	Ellery Hanley	(Bradford)
45	Gary Prohm	(Hull K.R.)
34	Henderson Gill	(Wigan)
30	Barry Ledger	(St.Helens)
28	Mal Meninga	(St.Helens)
27	Vince Gribbin	(Whitehaven)
26	Carl Gibson	(Batley)
25	Gary Peacham	(Carlisle)
25	Ged Byrne	(Salford)
24	Steve Evans	(Hull)
24	John Ferguson	(Wigan)

GOALS

157	Sean Day	(St.Helens)
141	George Fairbairn	(Hull K.R.)
126	Peter Wood	(Runcorn H.)
122	Graham Steadman	(York)
118	Clive Griffiths	(Salford)
117	Mick Parrish	(Oldham)
105	Garry Schofield	(Hull)
102	David Creasser	(Leeds)
87	Malcolm Agar	(Halifax)
87	Ken Jones	(Swinton)

Timeline
1986

(Above)
John Joyner lifts the Cup for Castleford at Wembley in 1986.

Rugby League got a sign of things to come ten years down the line when, early in 1986, the game had to tackle the threat of a breakaway 'Super League' following a secret meeting of 10 top clubs. Those leading clubs said they required more direct influence and control of the game, plus a bigger share of the financial rewards. Fears of a breakaway were allayed when the Rugby League Council agreed to a series of proposals, including the reduction of Division One to 14 clubs and cutting the levy on receipts paid by top clubs from 15% to 8%, along with an increased share of sponsorship prize money to successful clubs.

Meanwhile, the Amateur game finally saw some daylight in their quest to end Rugby Union's banning of those who had played League, when the Sports Council (which had previously been influenced by officials from Rugby Union backgrounds) got a new Chairman in John Smith, formerly of Liverpool Football Club, who vowed to resolve the problem. It was good news for the Amateur game which was thriving as BARLA launched their new 10-team National League in 1986, the first Student World Cup was staged, and numerous new developments continued to spring up all around the country.

(Above) **Brett Kenny became the second winner of the Golden Boot award in 1986, which he received whilst in Engand as a member of the Kangaroo touring team.**

National appreciation of the game was booming as the 1986 Kangaroo touring team arrived, aiming to emulate their famous unbeaten predecessors of four years earlier, and a British public eager to see them. The template for the tour was set when almost 31,000 people were at Wigan for the opening match, the biggest ever attendance for a tour match against a club side. The RFL showed their ambitions by staging the first Ashes Test match at Old Trafford, the home of Manchester United, and were rewarded in quite spectacular style when a crowd of 50,583 turned up, a record for an international match in Britain. They, along with a nationwide live television audience of several millions, saw Australia produce a masterclass of Rugby League, leaving Britain's Ashes hopes shattered once again, despite the individual brilliance of the likes of Joe Lydon and Garry Schofield.Lydon had become the first player to command a straight £100,000 transfer fee early in the year when he moved to his home town club Wigan from Widnes.

The world of sport in 1986

Argentina, inspired by captain Diego Maradona, win the football world club staged in Mexico. Mardona's 'hand of God' (no) goal helps knock England out controversially in the quarter-final.
* With English clubs banned from Europe after the Heysel Stadium tragedy, Liverpool complete a Cup and League double at home.
* A 20-year-old American, Mike Tyson, wins the heavyweight boxing title for the first time.
* West Indian batsman Viv Richards scores 100 off just 56 balls in a Test annihilation of England.
* Australian golfer Greg Norman wins the British Open for the first time, after many years of trying.
* Chicago Bears win the NFL's Superbowl with a record 46-10 win over New England Patriots.

The New Zealand coach Graham Lowe had joined Wigan before the 1986-87 season as the cherry and whites' strength continued to grow - but Wigan couldn't get their hands on either of the two top trophies in 1986 as Yorkshire clubs Castleford and Halifax won Challenge Cup and Championship respectively. Castleford, coached by Malcolm Reilly, and with a team mostly of locals, beat favourites Hull K.R. in a tense Wembley final. The Robins were handicapped by their star Aussie loose-forward Gavin Miller going into the game unfit. There was a much happier conclusion to the season for another Australian, Chris Anderson, who player-coached Halifax to the Championship. It was a remarkable turnaround in fortunes for Halifax, whose president David Brook had recruited five Australians in his quest to bring success and the crowds back to Thrum Hall. A sad moment for the game in 1986 was the death of former t.v. commentator Eddie Waring in October, at the age of 76.

(Above, left) Joe Lydon, the game's first £100,000 cash transfer, bursts through a tackle by Wally Lewis as the 1986 Kangaroo tour kicked off with a thriller against Wigan. (Above, right) Chris Anderson leads the Halifax attack. The Australian player-coach did a remarkable job in bringing the Championship title back to Thrum Hall for the first time in 31 years.

TOP TEN

1985-86
TRIES
49	Steve Halliwell (Leigh)
38	Ellery Hanley (Wigan)
34	Peter Lister (Bramley)
31	John Henderson (Leigh)
30	Tommy Frodsham (Blackpool)
29	Phil Fox (Leigh)
27	Stewart Williams (Barrow)
24	Brian Garrity (Runcorn H.)
23	Carl Gibson (Leeds)
23	David Beck (Workington)

GOALS
173	Chris Johnson (Leigh)
128	David Stephenson (Wigan)
118	David Noble (Doncaster)
115	Kevin Harcombe (Rochdale)
110	Shaun Kilner (Bramley)
101	John Dorahy (Hull K.R.)
98	John Woods (Bradford N.)
84	David Creasser (Leeds)
83	Dean Carroll (Carlisle)
83	Gary Smith (Workington)

(Above) Drama at Wembley in 1986 as Hull K.R.'s John Dorahy takes a last minute conversion attempt from the touchline which, if successful, would have won the Cup. To the despair of the Robins, the kick missed and Castleford prevailed to win the Cup 15-14.

Timeline
1987

(Right)
One of the classic images of 1987 as Halifax full-back Graham Eadie leaves St.Helens defenders in his wake as he bounds over under the posts for a try in the Challenge Cup Final. The former Australian Test full-back Eadie had come out of retirement to join Halifax and fully justified their gamble. He defied a hamstring injury at Wembley to help Halifax to their thrilling 19-18 win over St.Helens, and was awarded the Lance Todd Trophy. It crowned a wonderful two years for Halifax as they added the Cup to the Championship they had won in 1986.

Rugby League enjoyed its first ever £1million gate in 1987 as Halifax won the Challenge Cup for the first time in 48 years. Led by player-coach Chris Anderson, who celebrated his 35th birthday as he lifted the trophy at Wembley, the game enjoyed another sensational day under the twin towers as a crowd of 91,267 saw a nail-biting contest. It was a popular triumph for Halifax, who had only been promoted from the Second Division in 1984. Halifax were succeeded as Champions in 1987 by Wigan, winning their first title for 27 years, as a new dynasty was being established at Central Park under the guidance of former Kiwi coach Graham Lowe.

In his first season at Wigan, Lowe saw his team win every major trophy except the Challenge Cup - this included their first Premiership title triumph in the year the final was first played at Old Trafford. Later in the year in the early weeks of the 1987-88 campaign, Wigan enjoyed even greater glory when they took on, and defeated, the Australian Premiership winners Manly, to be crowned World Club Champions on a magnificent night at a Central Park packed to the rafters with a crowd

The world of sport in 1987

* Coventry City win the F.A.Cup, beating Spurs in the Final at Wembley, 3-2 after extra time.
* Rugby Union stages its very first World Cup some 33 years after Rugby League pioneered the way. New Zealand's All Blacks win on home soil, beating France 29-9 to win the Webb Ellis Trophy.
* 'Sugar' Ray Leonard wins boxing's middleweight world title by ending Marvin Hagler's seven year reign as champion in Las Vegas.
* Lincoln City become the first team to be automatically relegated from the Football League. Previously the team which finished bottom of all four divisions could apply for re-election.
* England cricket captain Mike Gatting has an angry exchange with an umpire in a Test match in Pakistan.

of almost 37,000. Earlier in 1987 Wigan had continued to show their ability to attract the game's best talent when they set a new cash transfer-fee record of £130,000 signing Andy Gregory from Warrington. In August that was surpassed by Leeds paying Hull £150,000 for Lee Crooks, and again in October when they paid £155,000, also to Hull, for Garry Schofield. Despite this continued boom in transfer fees, major changes were ahead as a new players' contract system was intro-

duced in the summer of 1987 - it was a radical move which would change Rugby League dramatically as players could arrange their own contracts and were no longer tied to one club indefinitely.

It was a very busy autumn of international rugby as Britain hosted Papua New Guinea, making their second tour to Europe but the first where they met professional opposition in England, including a full Test match against Great Britain. The British side, now coached by Malcolm Reilly, won the Test comfortably, 42-0. The Auckland team from New Zealand also made a six match tour, and they were quickly followed by the Junior Kiwis whose tour was hosted by BARLA. On the home front, many clubs were struggling more and more to meet the requirements of new ground safety regulations, prompted by the Bradford fire in 1985. In February 1987, RFL secretary David Oxley criticised some local authorities who were being less than helpful, and the club most severely hit was Blackpool Borough. After much wrangling, Blackpool's ability to stay at their Borough Park ground proved impossible, and the club moved to become Springfield Borough, playing at the Wigan Athletic football ground in 1987-88. It was also in 1987 that the Sports Council mediator in the dispute between the RFL and BARLA over youth rugby recommended scrapping the RFL's Colts teams.

(Above, left) Aussie wing Andrew Ettingshausen at full pace for Leeds in the 1987 Challenge Cup against Barrow. *(Above, right)* In the one season of Springfield Borough, Bob Eccles and Danny Wilson get to grips with an opponent at Carlisle. *(Left)* Doncaster's David Noble, who was third top goal-kicker in the Rugby League in 1986-87 as the Dons achieved a very creditable fourth place in the Second Division.

TOP TEN

1986-87

TRIES

63	Ellery Hanley	(Wigan)
37	Garry Schofield	(Hull)
32	Henderson Gill	(Wigan)
31	Derek Bate	(Swinton)
30	Phil Ford	(Bradford N.)
27	John Henderson	(Leigh)
26	Shaun Edwards	(Wigan)
25	Brian Johnson	(Warrington)
24	Joe Lydon	(Wigan)
23	Brian Dunn	(Rochdale H.)
23	Barry Ledger	(St.Helens)
23	Kevin McCormack	(St.Helens)

GOALS

190	Paul Loughlin	(St.Helens)
117	Paul Bishop	(Warrington)
114	David Noble	(Doncaster)
109	Colin Whitfield	(Halifax)
102	Alan Platt	(Hunslet)
100	Paul Topping	(Swinton)
86	Chris Johnson	(Leigh)
80	Martin Ketteridge	(Castleford)
80	David Wood	(Rochdale H.)
77	Steve Quinn	(Featherstone)

Timeline
1988

(Above)
Martin Offiah - the game's new sensation in his first season in Rugby League - pictured in his Test debut in France in January 1988, and at Naughton Park scoring one of his 42 Widnes tries which set a new seasonal record for the Chemics.

Rugby League was feeling very good about itself in 1988 - with a major increase in attendances recorded during the 1987-88 season as the First Division championship, now reduced from 16 to 14 clubs, showed a 20% rise in average crowds. An even bigger 40% increase came in the Second Division which had grown from 18 to 20 clubs. This boom at the turnstiles was matched by ever increasing sponsorship deals, mainly from breweries as Stones Bitter backed the Championship & Premiership, Whitbread the Great Britain teams and internationals matches, and John Smiths and Grunhalle Lager the Yorkshire and Lancashire Cups respectively. The Whitbread company took their support even further by backing the creation of the new Rugby League 'Hall of Fame' - based at Oulton, near Leeds, it was opened in October 1988 with a special ceremony at which nine founder members were inducted: Billy Batten, Brian Bevan, Billy Boston, Alex Murphy, Jonty Parkin, Gus Risman, Albert Rosenfeld, Jim Sullivan and Harold Wagstaff. To celebrate the launch of the 'Hall of Fame' Whitbread sponsored a special match between Great Britain and a Rest of the World team, and a crowd of 12,409 attended at Headingley to see an entertaining encounter won narrowly by the home team, 30-28, the match also being televisied live by the BBC.

By early 1988 it was obvious the game had a new star in the shape of Martin Offiah. Widnes manager Doug Laughton signed the young winger from Rosslyn Park Rugby Union club in the summer of 1987, and he was an instant success. Offiah finished his first season as the game's top try-scorer, which included setting a new Widnes club record for tries in a season. He made a try scoring debut for Great Britain as they won in France in January 1988 - and although Offiah was left out of the return Test with France,

The world of sport in 1988

*Wimbledon shock the football world by winning the F.A.Cup, just 11 years after rising from the Southern League. They beat Liverpool in the Final at Wembley with a goal by Lawrie Sanchez.
* At the Olympic Games in Seoul, Canadian sprinter Ben Johnson is stripped of his 100 metres gold medal after being found to be a drugs cheat.
* West German tennis star Steffi Graf wins the Grand Slam of all four major titles, before going on to win gold at the Seoul Olympics as tennis returns to the games after an absence of 64 years.
* 'Sugar' Ray Leonard just manages to hold onto his WBC middleweight title after a bruising drawn fight with Thomas 'the Hit Man' Hearns.
* Severiano Ballesteros wins his third British Open gold championship at Lytham and St.Annes

(Above) **The four living founder members of the 'Hall of Fame' - Alex Murphy, Gus Risman, Brian Bevan and Billy Boston - pictured at the official opening at Oulton, near Leeds, in October 1988.**

David Plange being chosen instead, the Widnes flyer became a Lions tourist in 1988. The Ashes were lost again on that tour and the British could only look on as New Zealand got to stage a World Cup Final against Australia. Offiah's Widnes won a double of Championship and Premiership, whilst Chris Anderson's successful era with Halifax came to a close with another Wembley final, won in stunning style by Wigan in front of a capacity 94,273 - the last of the mega crowds before Wembley's change to all-seater meant a reduction to 78,000. In April 1988 Tom O'Donovan became Rugby League's first National Development Officer, and in November Fred Lindop was appointed Referees' Controller. Disaster struck for Dewsbury in September when fire destroyed the grandstand at Crown Flatt.

(Above) **Whitehaven loose-forward Milton Huddart in action against Batley in November 1988, with New Zealander Dave Watson and Martin Amor in support. Huddart, who played for England in 1984, was a subject of the new Transfer Tribunal when he returned to Whitehaven from Leigh in 1988 and a £10,000 fee was set - £25,000 less than Leigh were asking.**

TOP TEN

1987-88
TRIES

44	**Martin Offiah** (Widnes)
36	**Ellery Hanley** (Wigan)
25	**Garry Schofield** (Leeds)
24	**Carl Gibson** (Leeds)
23	**Andy Goodway** (Wigan)
23	**Kevin Pape** (Carlisle)
21	**Shaun Edwards** (Wigan)
21	**Des Foy** (Oldham)
21	**Peter Smith** (Featherstone)
20	**Chris Bibb** (Featherstone)
20	**Mark Conway** (Wakefield)
20	**Mark Elia** (St.Helens)
20	**Les Quirk** (St.Helens)

GOALS

152	**John Woods** (Warrington)
128	**Steve Quinn** (Featherstone)
116	**Kevin Harcombe** (Wakefield)
114	**Paul Loughlin** (St.Helens)
111	**Gary Pearce** (Hull)
98	**Mike Smith** (Springfield Boro)
95	**David Stephenson** (Leeds)
94	**Mike Fletcher** (Hull K.R.)
83	**David Hobbs** (Bradford N.)
79	**Ken Jones** (Salford)

(Above) **Hugh Waddell giving a strong display for Great Britain in their 30-12 win over France at Headingley in February 1988, as the French hooker Mathieu Khedimi tries to halt his progress. Waddell, formerly of Blackpool Borough, was an Oldham player at the time but was signed by Leeds after his impressive Lions tour in 1988.**

Timeline
1989

The last year of the 'eighties saw Wigan and Widnes maintain their dominance of club Rugby League in England - Wigan retaining the Challenge Cup and Widnes their Championship and Premiership double. And big money continued to flow through a sport now full of self confidence and enjoying very successful times as transfer fees hit new heights and lucrative deals were offered to Rugby Union players as well as ready-made League stars from Australia. No individual signing attracted more publicity that the Welshman Jonathan Davies when he became a Widnes player in January 1989. He was eased into the game gently by Chemics coach Doug Laughton amid a frenzy of media attention, and in the time honoured fashion of learning the game from the wing Davies was able to share in Widnes victories in a wonderful Championship decider against Wigan and their Premiership Final win over Hull at Old Trafford. The Manchester United ground was also the venue in October for an even greater Widnes triumph as they swept aside the Australian champions Canberra Raiders to be crowned World Club Champions. On the other wing for Widnes that night, and scorer of a spectacular try, was Martin Offiah - who completed his second season in the game with a try haul of 60 and firmly established as one of the best known personalities in British sport.

Offiah was one of a large group of top British players who were in demand from Australian clubs in 1989, and they spent the off-season down-under. Among them was Ellery Hanley who became the first British winner of the Golden Boot award and also flew from Sydney to Milwaukee in the USA to captain Wigan in their exhibition match against Warrington. With big spending Wigan and Widnes at the top, and so many stars in their ranks, it was perhaps surprising that a new world record transfer fee was set in deal between two local Yorkshire rivals as Castleford paid Featherstone Rovers £170,000 for Graham Steadman. Rovers were confident they had new talent coming through and none was better than the teenage centre Paul Newlove who had taken the game by storm. Newlove became Great Britain's youngest ever Test player (aged 18

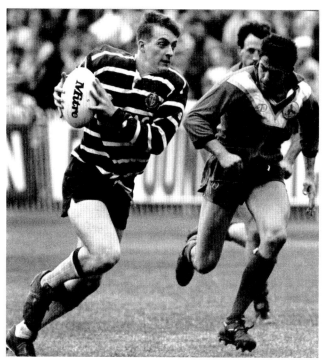

(Above) **Two of the best emerging talents of 1989 in action as Paul Newlove of Featherstone Rovers is chased by Daryl Powell of Sheffield. Newlove became Britain's youngest ever Test player in 1989.**

The world of sport in 1989

* Tragedy strikes football again as 95 fans are killed in an horrific crush at Sheffield Wednesday's Hillsborough ground during an F.A.Cup semi-final between Liverpool and Nottingham Forest.
* Liverpool emerge from the Hillsborough disaster to win the F.A.Cup, beating neighbours Everton in the Final at Wembley, 3-2 after extra time..
* Arsenal clinch football's First Division title with a late goal by Michael Thomas in the last match of the season, a 2-nil win over Liverpool at Anfield.
* British boxer Frank Bruno loses to Mike Tyson in the fifth round as he challenges for the world title.
* Peter Scudamore becomes the first National Hunt jockey to ride over 200 winners in a season.
* In Rugby Union, the British Lions play a three Test series in Australia for the first time, winning 2-1 under the captaincy of Scot Gavin Hastings.

years and 72 days) when he made his debut at Old Trafford, Manchester in the first Test of the 1989 series against New Zealand. The Kiwis won that day but Great Britain came back to win the series in dramatic style, a victory which was welcomed with great delight as the first home Test series win since the 1965 Kiwis were beaten on British soil. More international joy came as the second Student World Cup was staged in Britain, with the teams based in York, and the Minster City was also in the news as their Rugby League club moved out of the Clarence Street ground to a new stadium. Hull K.R. did the same, vacating the old Craven Park for the new model as the far reaching effects of the 1985 Bradford fire continued to be felt. As the Mansfield Marksman's struggles saw them metamorphose into Nottingham City in 1989, at least one of the game's 'new' clubs, Sheffield Eagles, had made significant progress. At the end of their fifth season in the game, the Eagles won their first trophy by capturing the Second Divison Premiership at Old Trafford in May 1989. Later in the year they also produced their first international when Daryl Powell was called up to the Great Britain squad, and were able to draw a crowd of over 8,500 at Bramall Lane to see them thrash the newly crowned World Champions, Widnes, 31-6. The Eagles had well and truly landed in 1989.

(*Above*) Images from 1989 as (*left*) Jonathan Davies runs the gauntlet of the media and young fans on the day he made his debut for Widnes at Naughton Park. (*Centre*) Gary Stephens as player-coach of York in their last season at Clarence Street before moving to a new stadium to become Ryedale-York. (*Right*) Phil McKenzie, a key part of the Widnes attacking machine which won the Championship, Premiership and World Club Challenge against Canberra.

TOP TEN

1988-89
TRIES
60	Martin Offiah (Widnes)
34	Barry Ledger (Leigh)
32	Derek Bate (Swinton)
29	Ellery Hanley (Wigan)
28	Peter Lister (Bramley)
28	Darryl Powell (Sheffield)
26	Peter Lewis (Bramley)
24	Les Quirk (St.Helens)
24	Grant Anderson (Castleford)
24	Paul Burns (Barrow)

GOALS
148	Mark Aston (Sheffield)
129	Martin Ketteridge (Castleford)
118	David Hobbs (Bradford N.)
117	Chris Johnson (Leigh)
115	Dean Marwood (Barrow)
113	Paul Loughlin (St.Helens)
110	David Noble (Doncaster)
107	John Woods (Warrington)
107	Andy Currier (Widnes)
104	Steve Turner (Rochdale H.)

(*Above*) Great Britain winger Phil Ford on a weaving run against New Zealand captain Hugh McGahan in the third Test in 1989 at Wigan. Great Britain won a thriller 10-6 to clinch the series.

TRINITY AND THE GREATS

Wally Lewis   Mark Graham

(Above) Steve Ella, a 1982 'Invincible', also played for Wakefield Trinity in 1988-89.

Many English clubs had a massive influx of players from down-under during the 1980s, but no team managed to sign bigger names than Wakefield Trinity who saw two of the decade's greatest figures don their red, white and blue colours. Both Wally Lewis and Mark Graham played for Trinity in what were sensational coups for the Wakefield club - as the captains of Australia and New Zealand respectively, Lewis and Graham were at the pinnacle of the international game throughout much of the 'eighties and have gone down in history as two of the all-time greats. It was remarkable that Wakefield managed to sign them ahead of all the wealthier and more successful clubs, as throughout the decade Trinity did not win any of the major trophies and often were in a struggle (sometimes in vain) to avoid relegation.

Wally Lewis's ten game spell with Trinity in the winter of 1983-84 has gone down in the game's folklore. A crowd of 8,179 saw his debut at Belle Vue against Hull on 4th December 1983 (none of Wakefield's previous five home games had attracted more than 3,000 spectators) and his impact on the team was immense. In contrast, Mark Graham was signed on a two year contract during the summer of 1988; the former Kiwi skipper was then 31-years-old and his great career with North Sydney had come to an end. Struggling against an ankle injury Graham called a halt to his career after just 14 appearances for Wakefield and went home in December 1988. During his time in England he also captained the World X111 against Great Britain.

MAGICAL MEMORIES

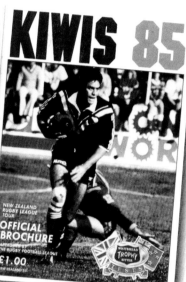

(Left) Leigh proudly show off the Championship trophy at Hilton Park in 1982.

(Left, below) Halifax centre Tony Anderson on the run against Warrington in the 1986 Premiership Final.

(Below) Brochures produced by *'Open Rugby'* to promote the tours in 1985 and 1986.

(Left) In the shadow of the tower, John Holdsworth gets to grips with Blackpool in their season as the 'Milers' as they met new boys Cardiff.

(Left, below) The John Player Trophy, won by Warrington in 1981.

(Left) Kevin Tamati being told to calm down in a fierce battle between Widnes and Warrington. No sign of Greg Dowling on this occasion for K.T.

LIONS ON TOUR 1984

(Above) Mike O'Neill, with Kevin Beardmore in support, makes a powerful run for the 1984 Lions in a tour game in Queensland. *(Right)* On the Lions' bench during their 14-8 win over the North Sydney club played at the Sydney Cricket Ground - coach Frank Myler, team manager Dick Gemmell and 'fitness director' Rod McKenzie.

(Above) Brian Noble, captain of the 1984 Lions touring team.

Faced with the task of rebuilding some British pride after the debacle of the 1979 tour and the 1982 Ashes whitewash by the 'Invincible' Kangaroos, the 1984 Lions touring team travelled down-under with a young side already showing improved levels of fitness. They came home with an unwanted and unprecedented record of failure in the Test matches, becoming the first ever British touring side to be whitewashed three-nil in the series in both Australia and New Zealand - but the new breed of young players in the Lions squad provided plenty of positive signs for the future. The 1984 touring team had an average age of 23, had the youngest ever Lions captain in 23-year-old hooker Brian Noble, and included the youngest ever tourist in the 18-year-old Garry Schofield who had just completed his first season as a professional player. The 12-week, 24 match tour also saw the British team carry a sponsor's logo on their jerseys for the first time as they were backed by the Harrogate based company Modern Maintenance Products. Coach of the touring team was Frank Myler, then the coach of Oldham and the last man to captain Britain to the Ashes in 1970, whilst Dick Gemmell was a controversial appointment as the team manager after being business manager on the previous tour in 1979 which recorded an unprecedented loss of over £30,000. Gemmell attracted more criticism for his performance on the 1984 tour, although this one was able to record a handsome profit thanks to the diligence of business manager, the RFL's Finance Officer Roland Davis. The Great Britain team was badly hit by injuries, starting when centre Ronnie Duane had his tour ended by a knee injury after just eight minutes of the opening match in Darwin, and the media corps travelling with the Lions were left dumbfounded by several Test selections which saw the emerging star Ellery Hanley put out onto the wing with Bradford full-back Keith Mumby at centre. Despite all this, captain Noble - who stepped into the role when original selection Trevor Skerrett was forced out of the tour by injury - led his team to play with plenty of fire against Australia, without seriously looking like winning the Tests. Indeed, they had to wait until their debut in Papua New Guinea to finally record a Test win.

TOUR RECORD

First match: 18th May 1984.
At Darwin - v Northern Territory.
Last match: 5th August 1984.
At Mount Hagen - v Papua N.G.
In Australia:
Played 15; Won 11; Lost 4.
Lost Test series: 3-0.
In New Zealand:
Played 8; Won 4; Lost 4.
Lost Test series: 3-0.
In Papua New Guinea:
Played 1; Won 1; Lost 0.
Won sole Test match.
Tour totals:
Played: 24; Won 16; Lost 8.

TEST RESULTS

At Sydney:
AUSTRALIA beat G.B. 25-8.
At Brisbane:
AUSTRALIA beat G.B. 18-6.
At Sydney:
AUSTRALIA beat G.B. 20-7.
At Auckland:
NEW ZEALAND beat G.B. 12-0.
At Christchurch:
NEW ZEALAND beat G.B. 28-12.
At Auckland:
NEW ZEALAND beat G.B. 32-16.
At Mount Hagen

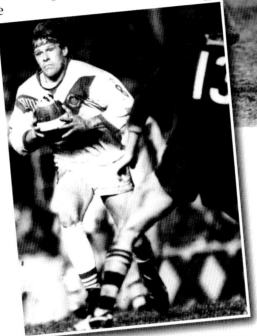

(Above) **Great Britain full-back Mick Burke on the attack in the third Test against Australia on the 1984 tour, is tackled by Eric Grothe with forward Greg Dowling covering.** *(Left)* **In the bruising second Test in Brisbane, British prop Keith Rayne carries the ball and is faced by Wayne Pearce, the Aussies' star loose-forward.**

THE 1984 LIONS

Mick Adams (Widnes)	**Joe Lydon** (Widnes)
Ray Ashton (Oldham)	**Keith Mumby** (Bradford)
Kevin Beardmore (Castleford)	**Tony Myler** (Widnes)
Mick Burke (Widnes)	**Brian Noble** (Bradford)
Chris Burton (Hull K.R.)	**Mike O'Neill** (Widnes)
Brian Case (Wigan)	**Harry Pinner** (St.Helens)
Garry Clark (Hull K.R.)	**Wayne Proctor** (Hull)
Lee Crooks (Hull)	**Keith Rayne** (Leeds)
Steve Donlan (Leigh)	**Garry Schofield** (Hull)
Des Drummond (Leigh)	**Mike Smith** (Hull K.R.)
Ronnie Duane (Warrington)	**Mick Worrall** (Oldham)
Terry Flanagan (Oldham)	*Replacement player:*
Des Foy (Oldham)	**John Basnett** (Widnes)
Andy Goodway (Oldham)	*(for Ronnie Duane)*
Andy Gregory (Widnes)	
Ellery Hanley (Bradford)	*Managers:*
David Hobbs (Featherstone)	**Mr. Dick Gemmell** (Hull)
Neil Holding (St.Helens)	**Mr. Roland Davis** (RFL)
John Joyner (Castleford)	*Coach:*
	Frank Myler (Oldham)

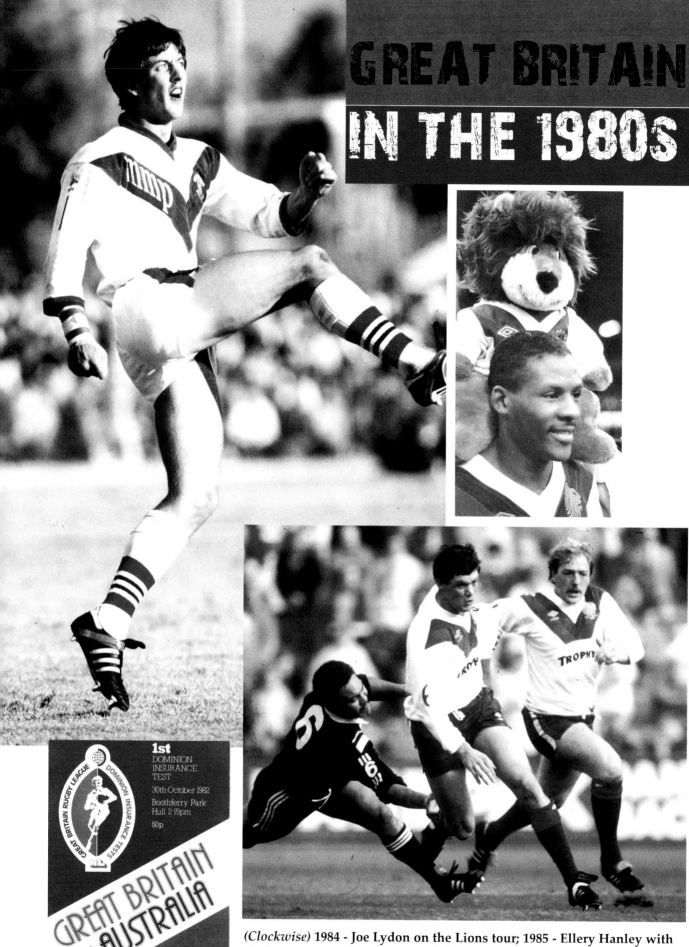

GREAT BRITAIN
IN THE 1980s

1st
DOMINION
INSURANCE
TEST

30th October 1982
Boothferry Park
Hull 2-15pm

50p

GREAT BRITAIN RUGBY LEAGUE · DOMINION INSURANCE TESTS · RL

GREAT BRITAIN v AUSTRALIA

Dominion Insurance
SPONSORS OF GREAT BRITAIN RUGBY LEAGUE

(Clockwise) 1984 - Joe Lydon on the Lions tour; 1985 - Ellery Hanley with 'Sully' the mascot; 1985 - Tony Myler on the attack with support from Mick Burke against New Zealand as Olsen Filipaina attempts to tackle; 1982 - Official programme for the pivotal first Ashes Test versus Australia at Boothferry Park, a day the earth moved for British Rugby League.

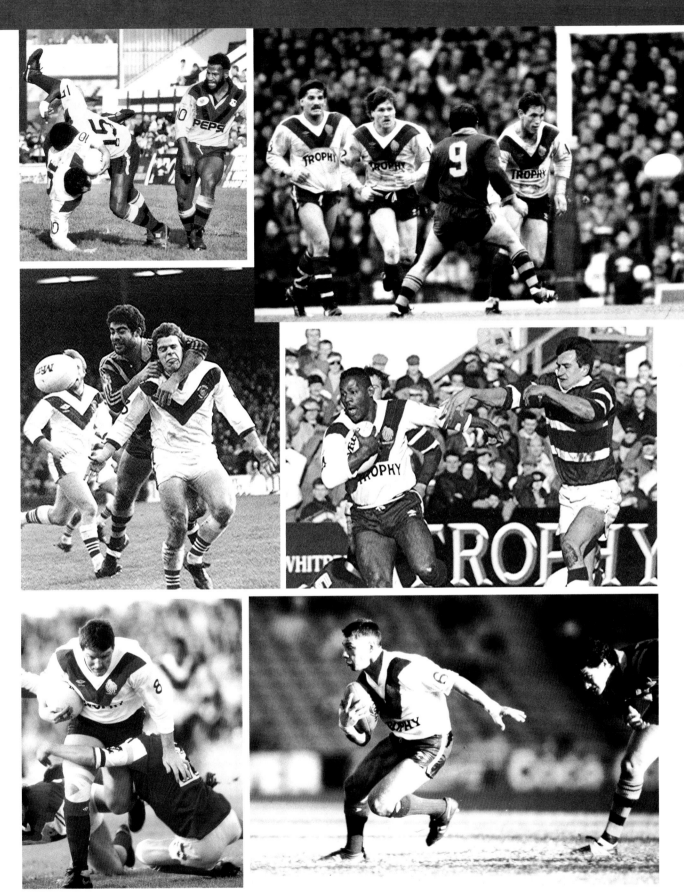

(Clockwise) **1987 - Crash landing for prop-forward Brian Case in Britain's first ever home Test with Papua New Guinea at Central Park; 1986 - Andy Goodway leads the charge against Australia at Old Trafford with Kevin Ward and Ian Potter in support; 1988 - Ellery Hanley evades France's full-back Jean-Phillipe Pougeau at Headingley; 1988 - David Hulme on the Lions tour beats Australia's Peter Jackson at the new Sydney Football Stadium; 1987 - David Hobbs tests France's tackling at Headingley; 1982 - Centre David Stephenson feels the mighty force of Mal Meninga as Great Britain were crushed by the 'Invincibles'.**

LIONS ON TOUR 1988

The 1988 Lions tour would rank as the most unsuccessful of any visit to the southern hemisphere by Great Britain were it not for one spectacular Test win over Australia. That came in the third match of the series, with the Ashes already retained by the Aussies, as a patched up Lions side -

ravaged by injuries and savaged by the Australian media - produced the performance of a lifetime to claim a 26-12 victory. Such had been the poor impression created by this Lions team up to that point, their famous triumph in Sydney on 9th July 1988 was watched by a record low crowd for an Ashes Test played in Australia, just 15,994 - among them a significant number of travelling British supporters who became ever more raucous as each of the Lions' five tries were scored and it became more obvious that Great Britain were going to record their first Test win over

(Above) **Captain Ellery Hanley scores in the first Test in Australia and is congratulated by Phil Ford and Martin Offiah.**

Australia for 10 years (since the famous so called 'Dad's Army' encounter at Odsal Stadium, Bradford in 1978).

As well as a huge boost for the British game's morale, that third Test victory in Sydney had the added bonus of being a World Cup qualifying match, and the two unexpected points gained by Great Britain meant their game in New Zealand the following weekend became a straight shootout semi-final with the British needing only a draw to then have the privilege of staging a World Cup Final on their own soil against Australia. Alas for the Lions, they lost to the Kiwis by just two points in the mud of Christchurch and the chance of massive event at a sold-out Old Trafford was gone.

Before that epic Test performance in the last match of the Australian leg of the tour, the 1988 Lions had endured one disappontment after another. Yet, in theory, this was the most meticulously prepared of any touring team to leave British shores, with a full-time coach in the person of Malcolm Reilly, a man hugely respected in Australia as well as his home

(Above) **Paul Loughlin scores a try in the opening minute of the Test in New Zealand which raised British World Cup hopes.**

land, and a back-up team including national coaching director Phil Larder and the vastly experienced Les Bettinson as team manager. Captained by Ellery Hanley, who made a massive impression on Australian pundits, so much so that he was recruited by Balmain to return and play for them immediately after the tour, much was expected of this British team, despite them

losing four of their first choice selections before their plane left Manchester. A lowlight of the tour was a 30-nil thrashing by Reilly's old Sydney club, Manly-Warringah, although Great Britain backed that up with a solid show in the opening Test - the first to be played at the new Sydney Football Stadium. After being rather unfortunate to lose the first Test, all hope was swept away with an undisciplined display in the second Test under the Lang Park lights, and the Ashes were gone once again. The 1988 Lions broke new ground by starting their tour in Papua New Guinea, but overall they finished with the unwanted record of seven defeats from 16 matches in Australia and New Zealand, the worst percentage since tours began to those two countries.

(Above)
In the first Test of the 1988 Ashes series at Sydney, Great Britain front-rower Kevin Ward slips out a trademark pass to scrum-half Andy Gregory, watched closely by skipper Ellery Hanley and the referee Mr. Francis Desplas.

TOUR RECORD

First game: 22nd May 1988.
At Port Moresby - v Papua new Guinea.
Last game: 19th July 1988.
At Carlaw Park, Auckland - v Auckland.
In Australia:
Played 13; Won 8; Lost 5.
Lost Test series: 2-1.
In New Zealand:
Played 3; Won 1; Lost 2.
Lost sole Test match.
In Papua New Guinea:
Played 2; Won 2; Lost 0.
Won sole Test match.
Tour totals:
Played 18; Won 11; Lost 7.

TEST RESULTS

At Port Moresby:
G.B. beat PAPUA NEW GUINEA 44-22.
At Sydney:
AUSTRALIA beat G.B. 17-6.
At Brisbane:
AUSTRALIA beat G.B. 34-14.
At Sydney:
G.B. beat AUSTRALIA 26-12.
At Christchurch:
NEW ZEALAND beat G.B. 12-10.

THE 1988 LIONS

Kevin Beardmore (Castleford)
Brian Case (Wigan)
Lee Crooks (Leeds)
Paul Dixon (Halifax)
Shaun Edwards (Wigan)
Karl Fairbank (Bradford)
Mike Ford (Oldham)
Phil Ford (Bradford)
Carl Gibson (Leeds)
Henderson Gill (Wigan)
Andy Gregory (Wigan)
Mike Gregory (Warrington)
Paul Groves (St.Helens)
Roy Haggerty (St.Helens)
Ellery Hanley (Wigan)
David Hulme (Widnes)
Paul Loughlin (St.Helens)
Paul Medley (Leeds)
Martin Offiah (Widnes)
Andy Platt (St.Helens)

Roy Powell (Leeds)
Garry Schofield (Leeds)
David Stephenson (Leeds)
Hugh Waddell (Oldham)
Kevin Ward (Castleford)
Ian Wilkinson (Halifax)
Replacement players:
Andy Currier (Widnes)
Richard Eyres (Widnes)
Paul Hulme (Widnes)
John Joyner (Castleford)
Darren Wright (Widnes)

Managers:
Mr. Les Bettinson (Salford)
Mr. David Howes (RFL)
Coach:
Malcolm Reilly
Assistant coach:
Phil Larder

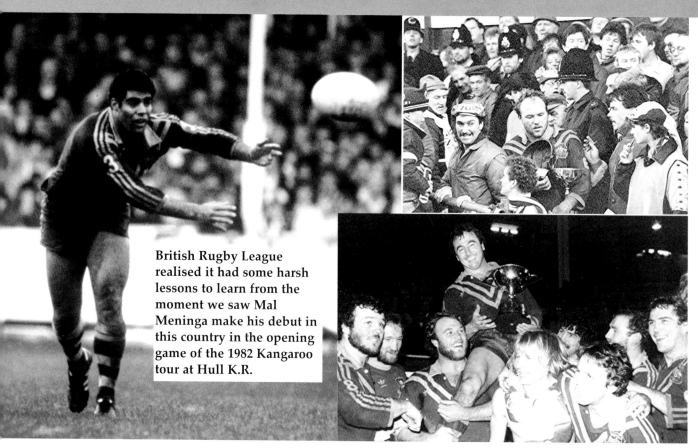

British Rugby League realised it had some harsh lessons to learn from the moment we saw Mal Meninga make his debut in this country in the opening game of the 1982 Kangaroo tour at Hull K.R.

SHOWING THE WAY

And the Aussies went on to storm to the Ashes undefeated in 1982 with Max Krilich and again in 1986 with Wally Lewis.

But the early warning signals were provided by the 1980 New Zealand touring team who played a popular brand of rugby as they drew the series with Great Britain, including a Test victory at Odsal after this haka.

THE YOUNG HOPEFULS

(Above) Great Britain Under-24s who beat France 19-16 at Leeds in January 1982. Left to right: (Back row): Ian Potter, Mike O'Neill, David Hobbs, Chris Arkwright, Ellery Hanley, David Stephenson, Mick Burke. (Front row): Andy Gregory, Des Drummond, Brian Noble, Barry Johnson, Henderson Gill and Andy Timson.

I n French sport they use the word *'Espoirs'* to describe teams at certain age levels, which translated into English means 'young hopefuls'. During the 1980s the 'young hopefuls' of British Rugby League, first at Under-24 level and later at Under-21, enjoyed much success over their counterparts from across the channel. As the Great Britain Under-24s, seven matches were played and all of them won, against the French *'Espoirs'* between January 1980 and December 1983. In that time period, the Under-24s lost only one match and that was against the New Zealand touring team in 1980 - going down 18-14 to the Kiwis in a game played at Fulham's Craven Cottage.

(Above) Wayne Proctor of Hull on attack for the British Under-24s against France at Villeneuve in 1983 - a 28-23 win for Great Britain. Mike O'Neill and Terry Flanagan are also pictured. (Left) Jimmy Dalton on home turf at Whitehaven for the Under-21s in 1986.

One of the first things Maurice Bamford did when he became Great Britain coach in the autumn of 1984 was have the age limit for these fixtures reduced to Under-21s. That led to much more competitive fixtures with the French, and in the ten games played at this level during the rest of the decade, Great Britain won six and France won four. And there was another very close match against the touring New Zealanders in 1985, the Kiwis winning 16-12 at Odsal. These games provided a great breeding ground for future Test players, and some of Great Britain's biggest stars of the decade - including Joe Lydon, Ellery Hanley, Garry Schofield, Tony Myler and Shaun Edwards - all played here before winning full caps.

(Above) Shaun Edwards playing stand-off for the Great Britain Under-21s in their 16-12 defeat to the Kiwis at Odsal in 1985. The British front row also in the picture are Andy Dannatt, Shaun Wane and Paul Groves (captain of the side).

GREAT BRITAIN REVIVAL

(Right)
A public show of patriotism from the Great Britain players at Wigan in 1985 before their stunning win over New Zealand. Captain Harry Pinner and Jeff Grayshon hold the Union Jack flag as John Fieldhouse and Shaun Edwards run alongside them.

(Above)
Coach Maurice Bamford and the Great Britain mascot 'Sully' the lion, enjoy a victory over the Kiwis in 1985.

The Great Britain team has always been the pinnacle of the Rugby League game for all its players and supporters, and during the 1980s they saw the profile of the international game grow to unprecedented heights - thanks to increased television coverage, new sponsorship support and a desperate desire to see the British team improve following the shock delivered to its system by the 1982 Kangaroos. From that nadir, Great Britain's stock had risen by the end of the decade to the point where it had won its first full three-match Test series on home soil since 1965, and it had also enjoyed one of its most epic Test match victories in Sydney in 1988 to end a ten year drought against Australia. The progress made in the six years between 1982 and '88 was perfectly captured by the image of back-row-forward Mike Gregory sprinting from his own half to score the final try for Great Britain in their 1988 win in Sydney with Wayne Pearce (the young forward whose athleticism had made him a star of the 1982 Kangaroo tour) being left in his slipstream. For the Lions assistant coach Phil Larder, who had done much to plot the British

(Above) The vivid and symbolic image of Mike Gregory leaving Australian star Wayne Pearce behind on the way to his try in the 1988 Test win in Sydney.

game's revival after 1982, it was a symbolic proof that we now had athletes to match even Wayne Pearce.

But it had been a long, hard road to get there and the Great Britain team had four coaches throughout the 1980s. The decade began with Johnny Whiteley at the helm as he tried to rebuild the British reputation after the disastrous 1979 Lions tour. Whiteley was coach against the 1980 Kiwis and the 1982 Kangaroos; after that Frank Myler took over the role in 1983 and '84, stepping down after the 1984 Lions tour in which all six Tests were lost in Australia and New Zealand. Myler was succeeded by Maurice Bamford who

Great Britain's Test Match record in the 1980s

Opponents	P	W	D	L
FRANCE	16	13	1	2
NEW ZEALAND	13	4	2	7
AUSTRALIA	12	1	0	11
PAPUA NEW GUINEA	3	3	0	0
Total	44	21	3	20

(Above) Great Britain line up at Headingley on 1st March 1985 with Maurice Bamford as coach for the first time, before hammering France by a record Test winning margin of 50-4. From the left they are: Les Bettinson (manager), Maurice Bamford (coach), Andy Goodway (captain), Shaun Edwards, Barry Ledger, David Creasser, Vince Gribbin, Henderson Gill, Ellery Hanley, Roy Dickinson, Deryck Fox, David Watkinson, Andy Dannatt, Alan Rathbone, Gary Divorty, Carl Gibson (sub.), Andy Platt (sub.). Phil Larder (assistant coach), Barry Gomersall (referee), the two touch-judges and Fred Lindop (reserve referee).

did a massive job in boosting morale by engaging the media and the wider public with his unbridled enthusiasm and passion for his country. Bamford had his British players running to the crowd holding the flag in the 1985 series against New Zealand which brought a credible draw against opponents who had just thrashed Australia, and did much to attract the record crowds which flocked to see the Tests against the 1986 Kangaroos. When Bamford stepped down after the 1986 Ashes, Malcolm Reilly was appointed full-time British coach and took preparation to a new level which led to, at last, a Test series win over New Zealand in 1989 - with the promise of greater things to come in the early 'nineties. Great Britain played a total of 44 Test matches during the 1980s, winning 21, losing 20 and drawing three. But it was sobering to note that against Australia, just one Test out of 12 was won, and against New Zealand there were seven lost, with four won and two drawn. In those 44 Tests Great Britain were led by 13 different captains, and there were four different companies providing sponsorship for the international team: at first it was Dominion Insurance, then M.M.P. for the 1984 Lions tour, Whitbread Trophy and by the end of the decade British Coal.

(Above)
Frank Myler as G.B. coach on the 1984 tour.

(Right)
A moment of glory for Great Britain coach Malcolm Reilly - flanked by assistant Phil Larder and Lions tour business manager David Howes - as the British beat the Australians in a Test match for the first time in ten years at Sydney in 1988.

1980s BRITISH TEST CAPTAINS

Tests	
13	Ellery Hanley
8	Brian Noble
4	Harry Pinner
4	David Watkinson
3	Len Casey
3	Mike Gregory
2	George Fairbairn
2	Jeff Grayshon
1	David Ward
1	Steve Nash
1	David Topliss
1	Keith Mumby
1	Andy Goodway

EURO INTERNATIONALS

(Right)
The last England team to be sighted in the 'eighties, pictured before their 28-9 win over Wales at Ebbw Vale in 1984. They are, left to right: *(Back row):* Des Drummond (Leigh), Milton Huddart (Whitehaven), Mick Burke (Widnes), David Hobbs (Featherstone), Andy Goodway (Oldham), Hugh Waddell (Blackpool), Ellery Hanley (Bradford), Andy Kelly (Hull K.R.). *(Front row):* Garry Schofield (Hull), Kevin Beardmore (Castleford), Steve Donlan (Leigh) captain, David Cairns (Barrow) and Garry Clark (Hull K.R.).

O nly two European Championships were played at the start of the decade before the resumption of full Test matches between Great Britain and France in 1981-82, but they produced two Anglo-French clashes which created enough controversy to last a lifetime. The trouble started at Narbonne in March 1980 when a big French crowd (estimated as many as 20,000 in some quarters) had come to see their team crowned Euro' champions after their convincing away win against Wales - instead they were thwarted by a brave England side (who won 4-2) and incensed by referee Billy Thompson. Ugly scenes followed the final whistle as Thompson had to run the gauntlet of an angry mob, and English officials were left fuming at the violence of certain French players, with some calling for Anglo-French internationals to be abandoned. France got their revenge the following year at Leeds, sending the highly controversial referee Guy Cattaneo to ensure their victory (5-1) which clinced the title and Jean Galia trophy for them. Although there were no more European Championships in the 'eighties, the birth of Cardiff Blue Dragons prompted a Wales-England match at Ninian Park in November 1981, which a full strength England won 20-15 in front of 8,102 spectators. Three years later, at Ebbw Vale, a new look English side again beat the Welsh, this time by 28-9.

EUROPEAN CHAMPIONSHIPS

1979-80
26th January 1980 - at Widnes.
Wales 7, France 21.
29th February 1980 - at Hull K.R.
England 26, Wales 9.
16th March 1980 - at Narbonne.
France 2, England 4.
Champions: England.

1980-81
31st January 1981 - at Narbonne.
France 23, Wales 5.
21st February 1981 - at Headingley.
England 1, France 5.
18th March 1981 - at Hull K.R.
Wales 4, England 17.
Champions: France.

Other internationals

8th November 1981 - at Cardiff.
Wales 15, England 20.
14th October 1984 - at Ebbw Vale.
Wales 9, England 28.

(Above) **Action from the two England-France clashes at the start of the decade as** *(left)* **Harry Pinner, Brian Case and Ken Kelly get stuck into French forward Manu' Caravaca at Headingley in 1981 as scrum-half Arnold Walker looks on; and** *(right)* **England forward Peter Gorley on the charge with John Joyner in support at Narbonne in 1980.**

FRENCH TESTS FOR BRITAIN

After several years of the European Championship involving England, France and Wales, full Test matches between Great Britain and France returned in the 1981-82 season. It was an indication of France's decline as a force in international Rugby League that the British managed to win 13 of their 16 Tests against them during the decade, with one match drawn. Many of those games were niggly affairs with the French still proving to be competitive (and much needed) opponents for Great Britain, although they did capitulate to three very heavy defeats on British soil, the worst in 1987 when the French game was in crisis. Neutral referees were at the helm of all these Tests in the 'eighties, and France's only two wins were officiated by two of Australia's most colourful referees, Greg Hartley and Barry Gomersall, both coming just two weeks after the French had been hammered by big scores away from home.

(Right) **John Woods is tackled by French forward José Giné as Great Britain won 37-0 at Hull in 1981 - Woods scoring seven goals and a try.**

(Above)
Vince Gribbin bounds over for one of Great Britain's eight tries in a record equalling 50-4 win over France at Leeds in 1985. Gribbin, a 19-year-old centre from Second Division Whitehaven, was one of 10 new caps selected by Great Britain coach Maurice Bamford.

GREAT BRITAIN - FRANCE TEST MATCHES IN THE 1980s

1981-82
6th December 1981 - at the Boulevard, Hull.
GREAT BRITAIN beat FRANCE 37-0. *Att.13,173.*
20th December 1981 - at Stade Velodrome, Marseille.
FRANCE beat GREAT BRITAIN 19-2. *Att. 6,500.*
1982-83
20th February 1983 - at Stade Domec, Carcassonne
GREAT BRITAIN beat FRANCE 20-5. *Att. 3,826.*
6th March 1983 - at the Boulevard, Hull.
GREAT BRITAIN beat FRANCE 17-5. *Att. 6,055.*
1983-84
29th January 1984 - at Parc des Sports, Avignon.
GREAT BRITAIN beat FRANCE 12-0. *Att. 5,000.*
17th February 1984 - at Headingley, Leeds.
GREAT BRITAIN beat FRANCE 10-0. *Att. 7,646.*
1984-85
1st March 1985 - at Headingley, Leeds.
GREAT BRITAIN beat FRANCE 50-4. *Att. 6,491.*
17th March 1985 - at Stade Gilbert Brutus, Perpignan.
FRANCE beat GREAT BRITAIN 24-16. *Att. 5,000.*

1985-86
16th February 1986 - at Parc des Sports, Avignon.
FRANCE & GT. BRITAIN drew 10-10. *Att. 5,000.*
1st March 1986 - at Central Park, Wigan.
GREAT BRITAIN beat FRANCE 24-10. *Att. 8,112.*
1986-87
24th January 1987 - at Headingley, Leeds.
GREAT BRITAIN beat France 52-4. *Att. 6,567.*
8th February 1987 - at Stade Domec, Carcassonne.
GREAT BRITAIN beat FRANCE 20-10. *Att. 1,968.*
1987-88
24th January 1988 - at Parc des Sports, Avignon.
GREAT BRITAIN beat FRANCE 28-14. *Att. 6,000.*
6th February 1988 - at Headingley, Leeds.
GREAT BRITAIN beat FRANCE 30-12. *Att. 7,007.*
1988-89
21st January 1989 - at Central Park, Wigan.
GREAT BRITAIN beat FRANCE 26-10. *Att. 8,266.*
5th February 1989 - at Parc des Sports, Avignon.
GREAT BRITAIN beat FRANCE 30-8. *Att. 6,500.*

THE KANGAROO TOURS

(Above) The 1982 Australian touring team line up at Headingley just a couple of days after arriving in the U.K. - from left to right: *(Back row):* John Ribot, Paul McCabe, Gene Miles, Donny McKinnon, Ian Schubert, Eric Grothe, John Muggleton, Craig Young, Greg Brentnall. *(Middle row):* Frank Stanton (coach), Mal Meninga, Rod Morris, Rohan Hancock, Rod Reddy, Les Boyd, Ray Brown, Greg Conescu, Ray Price, Brett Kenny, Wayne Pearce. *(Front row):* Alf Richards (trainer), Chris Anderson, Steve Mortimer, Steve Ella, Steve Rogers, Frank Farrington (manager), Max Krilich (captain), Tom Drysdale (co-manager), Wally Lewis (vice-captain), Peter Sterling, Kerry Boustead, Mark Murray and Bill Monaghan (doctor).

(Above) How *'Open Rugby'* commemorated the 1982 'Invincibles' tour with a special souvenir issue 'Kangaroos '82'.

1982

The 1982 Australian touring team have gone down in history as "The Invincibles" - the first touring side to go through both Britain and France undefeated and, in the process, set a new benchmark in the way the Rugby League game could be played. Yet these, the 15th Kangaroos, were roundly criticised before they left home soil as being an ordinary side, poorly selected with too many older players. Captained by Max Krilich, the veteran Manly hooker, they made the critics eat their words as they left Europe's best in their wake and had British fans drooling in admiration over the skills and athleticism they brought to the game.

The key man behind their success, based on a ruthless professionalism and attention to detail, was coach Frank Stanton - breaking the mould as the first man to coach successive Kangaroo touring teams. Stanton undoubtedly benefitted from the experience gained on the 1978 tour, most certainly when the Aussies went on to France for the second leg of their tour. This time there were to be no slip ups and, despite Australian encountering far more resistance from the French in the Tests than

(Above) **Coach Frank on the 1982 Kangaroo tour, with Steve Rogers standing close by.**

(Above) **Kerry Boustead outpaces Leeds winger Andrew Smith in the tour match at Headingley whilst Les Dyl grapples with Mal Meninga.** *(Above, right)* **Peter Sterling scores for Australia in the Second Test at Wigan, despite the efforts of Des Drummond to stop him. Kangaroo captain Max Krilich is in support.**

they had against Great Britain, they came through with a remarkable 100% record. The signs had been ominous in the tour's opening victory against Hull Kingston Rovers, when young stars - new to British audiences - Peter Sterling, Brett Kenny, Mal Meninga, Eric Grothe, Wally Lewis and Wayne Pearce - gave a hint of what was to come. Alongside more experienced campaigners like Rod Reddy, Ray Price, Les Boyd, Craig Young and Steve Rogers, the Aussies of 1982 developed into a footballing machine which won admiration from far beyond the world of Rugby League. They blew Great Britain away in the Ashes series, with their 40-4 thrashing of the home nation in the first Test at Boothferry Park sending shockwaves throughout the sport. This was the first Ashes series to be controlled by a referee from a neutral country, Frenchman Julien Rascagneres being the man in the middle. In the club games, the Aussies had particularly tough encounters with Wigan, Bradford and Hull as they strove to maintain their 100% record - but "The Invincibles" finished with a tour record of played 22, won 22, lost none - with 166 tries scored and only nine against them.

(Above) **Winger Eric Grothe celebrates his first Test try with delight from Wayne Pearce, Les Boyd and other team-mates.**

TOUR RECORD
First match: 10th October 1982. At Hull K.R. - v Hull K.R.
Last match: 16th December 1982. At Narbonne v France.
In Great Britain: Played 15; Won 15; Lost 0.
Won Test Series: 3-0.
In France: Played 7; Won 7; Lost 0.
Won Test Series: 2-0.

TEST RESULTS
At Boothferry Park:: **AUSTRALIA beat GT.BRITAIN 40-4.**
At Wigan: **AUSTRALIA beat GT.BRITAIN 27-6**
At Headingley: **AUSTRALIA beat GT. BRITAIN 32-6.**
At Avignon: **AUSTRALIA beat FRANCE 15-4.**
At Narbonne: **AUSTRALIA beat FRANCE 23-9.**

1982 KANGAROOS IN BRITAIN

October		Result		Att.
Sun. 10	Hull K.R.	Won	30-10	10,742
Wed. 13	Wigan	Won	13-9	12,158
Fri. 15	Barrow	Won	29-2	6,282
Sun. 17	St.Helens	Won	32-0	8,190
Wed. 20	Leeds	Won	31-4	11,570
Sun. 24	Wales	Won	37-7	5,617
Sat. 30	**GT.BRITAIN (1)**	**Won**	**40-4**	**26,771**
November				
Wed. 3	Leigh	Won	44-2	7,680
Sun. 7	Bradford	Won	13-6	10,506
Tues. 9	Cumbria	Won	41-2	5,748
Sun. 14	Fulham	Won	22-5	10,432
Tues. 16	Hull	Won	13-7	16,049
Sat. 20	**GT.BRITAIN (2)**	**Won**	**27-6**	**23,216**
Tues. 23	Widnes	Won	19-6	9,790
Sun. 28	**GT.BRITAIN (3)**	**Won**	**32-6**	**17,318**

THE KANGAROO TOURS

1986

(Right) **Mission was accomplished for the 1986 Kangaroos as captain Wally Lewis lifted the Ashes trophy following the third Test at Wigan. With a cleansweep in the Test series, and every other match on the tour won, Wally's 1986 side emulated their famous predecessors of 1982.**

(Below) **Winger Les Kiss on the run for the 1986 Kangaroos in their 40-nil thrashing of Leeds. In a tour of so many 'highs' and wonderful football, the one 'low' was the fate of Les Kiss, whose playing career was effectively ended by a knee injury sustained on the tour in the match against Widnes.**

The 1986 Kangaroo touring team faced their biggest challenge in trying to emulate the unbeaten record of their predecessors, "The Invincibles", four years earlier - and they stepped up to the plate in magnificent style. Despite facing the stronger challenge of a Great Britain side with a new breed of young stars more intensely prepared than ever before, the Australians of 1986 showed just how fast their game was moving ahead in the 'eighties.

Captained by Wally Lewis, who became the first Queenslander to lead a Kangaroo tour since Tom Gorman back in 1929, the 1986 Aussies brought just four other members of the '82 Invincibles back to Europe: Peter Sterling, Mal Meninga, Brett Kenny and Gene Miles. The latter, who had not been a Test player in 1982, firmly established himself as one of the most influential stars of the 1986 side. There were no forwards who had toured before and, to the great disappointment of the British public, two of the biggest stars from the 1982 tour were ruled out, very controversially, by injury - both Wayne Pearce and Eric Grothe left seething that they were forced to miss out when they considered themselves to be fit. The sixteenth Kangaroos were coached by Don Furner, whose easy-going approach was in sharp contrast to his 1982 predecessor Frank Stanton. Furner, aged 54, was coach at the Canberra Raiders and had toured before as a player 30 years earlier with the 1956 Kangaroos.

Such was the attraction of the 1986 Australian team, their tour in England was phenomenally successful. It opened when a wonderful crowd of over 30,000 packed into Central Park to see it start against Wigan (many of the local fans eager to welcome back Brett Kenny who had starred for them the previous year), and went on to produce a very healthy profit whilst creating more ground-breaking publicity for the Rugby League game. The first Test at Old Trafford, Manchester, drew a crowd of 50,583, the biggest ever to watch an international match in the U.K., with a world record

(Above) **Gene Miles after scoring a try in the opening Test in 1986 at Old Trafford, walks back alongside team-mates Brett Kenny and Mal Meninga - as disappointed British players and spectators look on.**

gate of £251,061. The Australian team's finances had already been boosted by an $88,000 sponsorship deal with the Winfield company and a $55,000 television deal with Channel 10 - whilst the British League enjoyed sponsorship backing from Whitbread company as the game headed into a new age of commercialism. After the opening match at Wigan, the Aussies' toughest club opponents were Oldham, who gave the tourists a real battle on a crisp night at the Watersheddings before going down 22-16, but in the Tests the Ashes were sown up after the first two games as Wally Lewis and his team produced some spectacular football. A much changed Great Britain team produced much sterner opposition in the third Test in which Australia needed the help of a couple of controversial refereeing decisions to complete their clean-sweep, skipper Wally Lewis putting the seal on it with a solo try. In France, the Kangaroos encountered little in the way of a challenge as they looked on sadly at the decline of the French game, both on and off the pitch, compared to previous years.

Don Furner, coach of the 1986 Kangaroos.

TOUR RECORD
First match: 12th October 1986. At Wigan - v. Wigan.
Last match: 13th December 1986. At Carcassonne v France.
In Great Britain: Played 13; Won 13; Lost 0.
Won Test Series: 3-0.
In France: Played 7; Won 7; Lost 0.
Won Test Series: 2-0.

TEST RESULTS
At Old Trafford: **AUSTRALIA beat GT.BRITAIN 38-16.**
At Elland Road: **AUSTRALIA beat GT.BRITAIN 34-4.**
At Wigan: **AUSTRALIA beat GREAT BRITAIN 24-15.**
At Perpignan: **AUSTRALIA beat FRANCE 44-2.**
At Carcassonne: **AUSTRALIA beat FRANCE 52-0.**

1986 KANGAROOS IN BRITAIN

October		Result		Att.
Sun. 12	Wigan	Won	26-18	30,622
Wed. 15	Hull K.R.	Won	46-10	6,868
Sun. 19	Leeds	Won	40-0	11,389
Tues. 21	Cumbria	Won	48-12	4,233
Sat. 25	**GT.BRITAIN (1)**	**Won**	**38-16**	**50,583**
Wed. 29	Halifax	Won	36-2	7,193
November				
Sun. 2	St.Helens	Won	32-8	15,381
Tues. 4	Oldham	Won	22-16	5,678
Sat. 8	**GT.BRITAIN (2)**	**Won**	**34-4**	**30,808**
Wed. 12	Widnes	Won	20-4	10,268
Sun. 16	Hull	Won	48-0	8,213
Tues. 18	Bradford	Won	38-0	10,663
Sat. 22	**GT.BRITAIN (3)**	**Won**	**24-15**	**20,169**

THE KIWI TOURS

(Right)
The 1980 Kiwi touring team pictured as they were introduced to the media at Salford. Left to right:
(Back row): Nolan Tupaea, Kevin Fisher, Ray Baxendale, Graeme West, John Whittaker, Gary Kemble, Ricky Muru, Barry Edkins.
(Middle row): Alan Rushton, Mike O'Donnell, James Leuluai, Mark Broadhurst, Bernard Green, Howie Tamati, Paul TeAriki, Bruce Gall, Bruce Dickison.
(Front row): Billy Kells, Tony Coll, Kevin Tamati, Cec Mountford (coach), Mark Graham (captain), Bill Nesbitt (manager), Fred Ah Kuoi, Dane O'Hara, Gary Prohm.
(In front): Gordon Smith and Shane Varley.

(Above) John Whittaker leads the 1980 Kiwis out for the first game of their tour at Blackpool.

T he 1980 New Zealand team, embarking on the first full Kiwi tour to Europe for nine years, arrived in England as a group of largely unknown young footballers. Many of them were destined to play with great success for both British and Australian clubs during the rest of the decade, and their exploits layed the foundation for a dramatic rise in the status of Rugby League in New Zealand. Furthermore, the style of football they played on the 1980 tour - based on fast moving support play and keeping the ball alive - acted as another firm 'wake up call' for the British game.

Much of the credit for that went to their manager-coach Cec Mountford, vastly experienced and a man from the 'old school' of Rugby League, who also did a lot to break down the Auckland domination of Kiwi teams with the 1980 touring squad including players from a wide variety of provinces. They were the last of the amateur tourists, with their squad of 26 players made up of 25 men from home-based New Zealand clubs plus one semi-professional in captain Mark Graham, who had moved to Australia to play in the Brisbane competition but was still working as a plasterer. It was whilst at the Kiwis' base in Harrogate on the 1980 tour that Graham agreed to join the North Sydney club and embark on his highly successful professional career. In total, 13 of this Kiwi touring went on to be signed by British clubs (including Mark Graham who finished his career with a brief spell at Wakefield Trinity in 1988) - with the two Hull clubs in particular having cause to thank them for many of their successes during the 'eighties. Only one of the 1980 squad was a survivor from the successful 1971 Kiwi touring team, the Wellington centre John Whittaker, and Cec Mountford's pre-tour assessment was that his young team were eager to learn. Cec also expressed the hope that the 1980 Kiwis would play attractive football to draw big enough crowds to ensure that the New

(*Left*) New Zealand front-rower Alan Rushton tackled by Les Gorley and Kevin Dick in the first Test as Steve Hartley looks on. (*Above*) The star of the 1980 Kiwi tour, Fred Ah Kuoi.

Zealand Rugby League did not make a financial loss on the tour. That ambition was achieved with crowds showing a 30% increase on the 1971 trip, which was staged at a time when the British game was at a very low ebb. The biggest attendance was at Boothferry Park in Hull, to witness the pivotal display of the 1980 tour as the young Kiwis swept aside one of England's most star-studded clubs, Hull F.C. with a style of football which had British critics drooling with admiration. That form was continued into the Test series, with a draw and then a victory making sure the series could not be lost by the Kiwis. Only the lack of a reliable goal-kicker prevented further success for one of the most popular touring teams ever to visit British and French shores.

(*Above*) Great Britain prop Roy Holdstock (of Hull K.R.) in action in the 1980 Second Test versus New Zealand - and, alongside, the programme for the 1980 first Test at Wigan.

TOUR RECORD
First match: 29th September 1980.
At Blackpool - v Blackpool Borough.
Last match: 7th December 1980.
At Toulouse - v France.
In Great Britain:
Played 14; Won 7; Drew 1; Lost 6.
Drew Test series: 1-1, with 1 match drawn.
In France:
Played: 7; Won 6; Lost 1.
Drew Test series: 1-1.

TEST RESULTS
At Wigan: **G.B. and NEW ZEALAND drew 14-14.**
At Bradford: **NEW ZEALAND beat G.B. 12-8.**
At Headingley: **G.B. beat NEW ZEALAND 10-2.**
At Perpignan: **FRANCE beat NEW ZEALAND 6-5.**
At Toulouse: **NEW ZEALAND beat FRANCE 11-3.**

1980 KIWIS IN BRITAIN

September		Result		Att.
Sun. 29	Blackpool	Won	23-5	1,312
October				
Sun. 5	Hull	Won	33-10	15,945
Wed. 8	Cumbria	Lost	3-9	4,398
Sun. 12	St.Helens	Lost	6-11	6,000
Tues. 14	Bradford N.	Lost	10-15	4,553
Sat. 18	**GT.BRITAIN (1)**	**Drew**	**14-14**	**7,031**
Wed. 22	Hull K.R.	Won	20-12	9,516
Sun. 26	Leeds	Won	25-5	5,662
Wed. 29	Warrington	Lost	7-11	5,680
November				
Sun. 2	**GT.BRITAIN (2)**	**Won**	**12-8**	**10,946**
Wed. 5	G.B.Under-24s	Won	18-14	2,397
Sun. 9	Widnes	Lost	7-14	6,416
Tues. 11	Leigh	Won	22-5	3,166
Sat. 15	**GT.BRITAIN (3)**	**Lost**	**2-10**	**8,210**

1985

(Above) **Clayton Friend in the Second Test on the 1985 Kiwi tour.**

In the five years which had passed since the Kiwis' previous tour in 1980, things had changed dramatically in New Zealand Rugby League. No longer almost exclusively amateur players from their own domestic competitions, the 1985 Kiwis had a backbone of hardened professionals with Australian clubs - among them their captain Mark Graham (one constant from the 1980 tour) Dean Bell, the enigmatic Olsen Filipaina and the rugged Sorensen brothers. In addition, for the first time New Zealand called up players from British clubs for the Test matches - seven in total: the Hull quartet of Kemble, Ah Kuoi, Leuluai and O'Hara; Hull K.R.'s Gary Prohm; Kevin Tamati of Warrington and Wigan's Graeme West. An inspirational young coach, Graham Lowe, had taken over the reins from Cec Mountford and created a massive impression in guiding the Kiwis to a famous win over Australia in Brisbane in 1983 and a three-nil Test whitewash of Great Britain in '84. Lowe's 1985 touring team arrived in Europe on the back of a a desperately unlucky loss in a three match series against the Aussies which had climaxed with an 18-nil World Cup triumph for New Zealand and took the game to new heights of public acclaim in their country. That made the Kiwis hot favourites to win the Tests in England, but the Great Britain team rose to the challenge to achieve a drawn series which did a massive amount to raise the morale of the British game.

Much of the Kiwis' hopes rested on the broad shoulders of their captain Mark Graham. He gave a magnificent virtuoso 40 minute performance in the first Test, before being forced off the field by an injury which also kept him out of the second Test in which the British team ran riot. New Zealand got Graham patched up enough to play in the deciding Test and his influence was crucial in a match that was often brutal, and included a host of controversial incidents, before finishing in a thrilling 6-all draw. The Kiwi captain did not go with the team on the French leg of their tour, but they had enjoyed a highly successful tour in England with crowds way up on the previous two tours by New Zealand.

(Above) **Captains Harry Pinner and Mark Graham share the trophy after the drawn series in 1985.**

1985 KIWIS IN BRITAIN

October		Result		Att.
Sun. 6	Wigan	Lost	8-14	12,856
Wed. 9	G.B.Under-24s	Won	16-12	2,285
Sun. 13	Hull K.R.	Won	20-10	6,630
Tues.15	Cumbria	Won	32-6	5,212
Sat. 19	**GT.BRITAIN (1)**	**Won**	**24-22**	**12,591**
Wed.23	Yorkshire	Lost	8-18	3,745
Sun. 27	St.Helens	Won	46-8	7,897
Tues.29	Leeds	Won	16-10	4,829
November				
Sat. 2	**GT.BRITAIN (2)**	**Lost**	**8-25**	**15,506**
Mon. 4	Widnes	Won	32-12	5,181
Sat. 9	**GT.BRITAIN (3)**	**Drew**	**6-6**	**22,209**
Wed.13	Lancashire	Cancelled		
Sun. 17	Hull	Won	33-10	8,406

TOUR RECORD
First match: 6th September 1985. At Wigan v Wigan.
Last match: 7th December 1985. At Perpignan v France.
In Great Britain: Played 12; Won 8; Drew 1; Lost 3.
(Match v Lancashire cancelled due to frozen pitch).
Drew Test Series: 1-1 with one match drawn.
In France: Played 7; Won 7; Lost 0.
Won Test Series: 2-0.

TEST RESULTS
At Headingley, Leeds: **NEW ZEALAND beat G.B. 24-22.**
At Wigan: **GT. BRITAIN beat NEW ZEALAND 25-8.**
At Elland Road, Leeds: **G.B. and N. ZEALAND drew 6-6.**
At Marseille: **NEW ZEALAND beat FRANCE 22-0.**
At Perpignan: **NEW ZEALAND beat FRANCE 22-0.**

T he third full Kiwi tour to Europe of the decade brought the disappointment for New Zealand of losing a Test series in Great Britain for the first time since 1965, although that loss was by an absolute whisker as they were defeated 10-6 in a thrilling final Test at Wigan which could so easily have gone their way. A touring side captained by the loose-forward Hugh McGahan and coached by Tony Gordon, lost only two other games in England apart from their two Test defeats, against St.Helens and Wigan, and created a good impression with their fast moving attacking football. As in 1985, the Kiwis had a solid based of professionals playing for Australian clubs, and in addition they called up the British based Dean Bell and Kurt Sorensen for three Test match appearances each.

New Zealand opened the Test series on new ground for them, with a convincing win at Old Trafford, the home of Manchester United. Stars in that victory included Kevin Iro and scrum-half Gary Freeman, and the latter unwittingly played a key role in the second Test when his being assaulted by opposing full-back Steve Hampson led to Great Britain playing a man short for 78 minutes of a game they rallied to win by a remarkable 26-6 margin. In the deciding Test, a low-scoring and unbearably tense game was, actually, full of sweeping attacks and expansive football, but the tackling of both sides was fierce and the Australian referee Greg McCallum caused no shortage of controversy for both sides, with the Kiwis particularly aggrieved as the chance of at least another drawn series slipped away from them.

Hugh McGahan's team attracted the highest aggregate crowds for a Kiwi tour in England since 1965 (when the tour consisted of 23 matches, almost double the 12 played in 1989) and the best for a Great Britain versus New Zealand Test series since 1961. Gary Mercer was chosen as New Zealand's best player in the three Test series and new stars, including Tawera Nikau and David Watson, made their bow on the international stage. When the Kiwis moved on to France they got a shock in the opening half hour of the first Test as the French side took a 14-nil lead, but New Zealand rallied to win 16-14 in a game switched at short notice to Carcassonne because the Perpignan pitch was waterlogged. There were no such dramas as the Kiwis powered their way to a 34-nil win in the second (World Cup rated) Test.

(Above) **David Watson on the attack for the 1989 Kiwis against Wigan, leaves his fellow New Zealander Dean Bell on the turf. Watson had made his name in the English game, first after being discoverd by Whitehaven and then at York, Bradford and Halifax, before being capped by his country for the first time in the second Test in France on the 1989 tour in which he scored a debut hat-trick of tries. He later played for Sheffield Eagles.**

TOUR RECORD

First match: 1st October 1989. At St.Helens v St.Helens.
Last match: 3rd December 1989. At Carcassonne v France.
In Great Britain: Played 12; Won 8; Lost 4..
Lost Test Series: 2-1.
In France: Played 5; Won 5; Lost 0.
(1 fixture unfulfilled due to Kiwis' failure to arrive on time)
Won Test Series: 2-0.

TEST RESULTS

At Old Trafford: **NEW ZEALAND beat G.B. 24-16.**
At Elland Road, Leeds: **G.B. beat NEW ZEALAND 26-6.**
At Wigan: **GT.BRITAIN beat NEW ZEALAND 10-6.**
At Carcassonne: **NEW ZEALAND beat FRANCE 16-14.**
At Carcassonne: **NEW ZEALAND beat FRANCE 34-0.**

1989 KIWIS IN BRITAIN

October		Result		Att.
Sun. 1	St.Helens	Lost	26-27	7,040
Tues. 3	Castleford	Won	22-20	5,993
Sun. 8	Wigan	Lost	14-24	15,013
Wed.11	Bradford	Won	26-8	3,498
Sun. 15	Leeds	Won	34-4	9,632
Tues.17	Cumbria	Won	28-2	3,983
Sat. 21	GT.BRITAIN (1)	Won	24-16	18,273
Sat. 28	GT.BRITAIN (2)	Lost	6-26	13,073
November				
Wed. 1	Featherstone	Won	44-20	2,773
Sun. 5	Widnes	Won	26-18	9,905
Tues. 7	Hull	Won	44-8	5,984
Sat. 11	GT.BRITAIN (3)	Lost	6-10	20,346

THE WORLD CUP

(*Above*) **Australian captain Wally Lewis, despite a broken arm, holds the World Cup after victory in the 1988 final in Auckland.** (*Above, right*) **Lewis leads his team against Papua New Guinea in their World Cup qualifying match played at Wagga Wagga.**

Only one World Cup was staged during the 'eighties, and it was a competition with a new format in which Test matches over a three year period were deemed as World Cup qualifiers. It gave an extra incentive in Tests series played in both hemispheres and, despite plenty of critics, it produced a thrilling climax and a massive final event. The tournament kicked off in Auckland in July 1985, and was completed in the same city over three years later in October 1988. Australia retained the title of World Cup winners they had held since the previous tournament back in 1977, but they suffered a couple of stunning defeats along the way, to the Kiwis in 1985 and against Great Britain in Sydney in 1988. That Lions victory provided an unexpected opportunity for the British to qualify for the World Cup Final, for which the Aussies had sacrificed home advantage - only a draw was needed by Great Britain in New Zealand, but the Kiwis prevailed by just two points and thus got to stage the biggest Rugby League event their nation had ever seen. A New Zealand record crowd of 47,363 packed into the Rugby Union citadel of Eden Park, and saw Australia outclass an indisciplined Kiwi side 25-12, despite losing their captain Wally Lewis with a broken arm. The 1985-88 World Cup was the first to include Papua New Guinea, and illustrated the crisis in the French game in 1987 when they had to forfeit their fixtures in the southern hemisphere.

WORLD CUP RESULTS

1985

July 7	Auckland	NEW ZEALAND 18, AUSTRALIA 0.
Nov. 9	Leeds	GREAT BRITAIN 6, NEW ZEALAND 6.
Dec. 7	Perpignan	FRANCE 0, NEW ZEALAND 22.

1986

Feb.16	Avignon	FRANCE 10, GREAT BRITAIN 10.
July 29	Brisbane	AUSTRALIA 32, NEW ZEALAND 12.
Aug.17	Port Moresby	PAPUA N.G. 24, NEW ZEALAND 22.
Oct. 4	Port Moresby	PAPUA N.G. 12, AUSTRALIA 62.
Nov.22	Wigan	GREAT BRITAIN 15, AUSTRALIA 24.
Dec.13	Carcassonne	FRANCE 0, AUSTRALIA 52.

1987

Jan.24	Leeds	GREAT BRITAIN 52, FRANCE 4
Oct.24	Wigan	GREAT BRITAIN 42, PAPUA N.G. 0.
Nov.15	Carcassonne	FRANCE 21, PAPUA N.G. 4.

1988

May 22	Port Moresby	PAPUA N.G. 22, GREAT BRITAIN 42.
July 9	Sydney	AUSTRALIA 12, GREAT BRITAIN 26.
July 10	Auckland	NEW ZEALAND 66, PAPUA N.G. 14.
July 17	Christchurch	NEW ZEALAND 12, GREAT BRITAIN 10.
July 20	Wagga Wagga	AUSTRALIA 70, PAPUA NEW GUINEA 8.

Final

Oct. 9	Auckland	NEW ZEALAND 12, AUSTRALIA 25.

AMERICAN DREAMS

The dream of taking Rugby League to the huge sports marketplace of the United States had been a recurring theme throughout the game's history since Harry Sunderland travelled with the 1921 Kangaroos across America. It was a dream which brought the name of Mike Mayer into the consciousness of the Rugby League world in 1977. Chicago born, Mayer was a big man who played college football for the University of Wisconsin and trialled for the New York Jets, and who fell in love with Rugby League after watching the film 'This Sporting Life'. The Australian Rugby League would not support Mayer's plans but the British Rugby League did invest significantly in his project in the late 'seventies and early 'eighties. However, it took him 12 years to get what he wanted: an exhibition game between two top professional teams on American soil, to act as a vehicle to promote the game via television to potential U.S. investors and supporters.

Mayer had been off the scene during the mid-'eighties, but caused the Australians much annoyance when they staged a match between Queensland and New South Wales in 1987 at Long Beach, California. He came back to England not long after that and managed to persuade Wigan supremo Maurice Lindsay to grasp the nettle of promoting the game in America, enlisting Wigan (and subsquently Warrington) to take part in an exhibition match billed as "The British Rugby League Football American Challenge" to be played at the County Stadium in Milwaukee, Wisconsin on 10th June 1989.

There were many hiccups and problems in getting the two teams to the starting gate, but it did take place - and a full bloodied encounter between the two arch rivals enthralled the American spectators, despite the players being restricted by a narrow pitch due to the baseball outfield. Wigan won 12-5 and both they and Warrington were given a five minute standing ovation at the end by a crowd offically announced as 17,773. In kits specially designed by Mike Mayer, incorporating the deep 'vees' he regarded as symbolic of Rugby League, the match was a very visually attractive event and the television highlights of it shown by the BBC did a massive job in promoting a more exciting image of the sport in Britain. Alas for Mayer, the match proved to be a financial disaster for him, as both Wigan and Warrington were left counting the cost of their investment which produced no return. It was the end of the road for the United States Rugby League, but the Milwaukee match in 1989 was a momentous event in the story of the game in the 'eighties.

(Above)
Action at Milwaukee in 1989 as *(left)* **Andy Goodway holds the ball aloft after scoring the only try of the game for Wigan, with captain Ellery Hanley alongside him; and** *(right)* **John Woods and Steve Hampson contest a high ball as Warrington's Les Boyd joins the action under the watchful eye of the referee John Holdsworth.**

(Above)
American Mike Mayer addresses schoolboys from England who had just played in a curtain-raiser at Milwaukee on 10th June 1989.

WORLD CLUB CHALLENGE

(Above, left) Flags fly and fireworks go off as Ellery Hanley leads Wigan out at a packed Central Park to play Manly in 1987. *(Middle)* Andy Gregory whips the ball away against Manly. *(Right)* Widnes stand-off Tony Myler evades Canberra's Laurie Daley as the Chemics emulated Wigan at Old Trafford in 1989.

(Above)
The Widnes trio of Martin Offiah, Joe Grima and Richard Eyres enjoy winning the World club title at Old Trafford in 1989.

Two of the big events which illustrated Rugby League's healthy state at the end of the 'eighties were the World Club Challenge games which saw English champions Wigan and Widnes take on, and beat, their Australian counterparts. It all started in 1987 when Wigan played Manly on an unforgettable night at a Central Park buzzing with excitement and packed to the rafters (just 105 short of its 37,000 capacity). Wigan won 8-2 in a tryless match, but there was never a dull moment as the teams went toe-to-toe - and it was a victory for home grown talent as every one of Wigan's players was English, with the sole exception of substitute Graeme West (their coach was Kiwi Graham Lowe).

Widnes, with Doug Laughton their coach, emulated Wigan's feat two years later when they beat Canberra Raiders, also with a large proportion of local Widnes lads in their team which was all British except for the trio of Sorensen, Grima and McKenzie. In 1987 Wigan had gone it alone and used their own enterprise to set up the Manly game, but by 1989 the RFL had accepeted the World Club Challenge under their wing and the game was staged at Manchester's Old Trafford ground. Widnes stormed back from an early 12-nil deficit to win with some spectacular attacking rugby.

1987
Wednesday 7th October, 1987 at Central Park, Wigan
Wigan 8, Manly-Warringah 2.
Wigan: Goals: Stephenson (4).
Manly-Warringah: Goal: O'Connor.
WIGAN: Hampson; Russell, Stephenson, Lydon, Gill; Edwards, Gregory: Case, Kiss, Wane, Goodway, Potter, Hanley. *Subs.:* Lucas (for Case), Byrne, West, Gildart.
MANLY: Shearer; Ronson, Williams, O'Connor, Davis; Lyons, Hasler; Daley, Cochrane, Gately, Gibbs, Cunningham, Vautin. *Subs.:* Shaw (for Cunningham), Brokenshire, Ticehurst, Pocock.
Referee: Mr. J. Holdsworth (Kippax, Nr. Leeds)
Attendance: 36,895.

1989
Wednesday 4th October, 1989, at Old Trafford, M'ster.
Widnes 30, Canberra Raiders 18.
Widnes: Tries: Offiah (2), Paul Hulme, Davies, Eyres, Wright. Goals: Davies (3).
Canberra: Tries: Meninga, O'Sullivan, Walters. Goals: O'Sullivan (2), Wood.
WIDNES: Tait; Currier, Davies, Wright, Offiah; Myler, D.Hulme; Grima, McKenzie, Pyke, Sorensen, P.Hulme, Eyres. *Subs.:* Dowd, Moriarty.
CANBERRA: Belcher; Wood, Meninga, Daley, Ferguson; O'Sullivan, Stuart; Jackson, Walters, Lazarus, Lance, Coyne, Clyde. *Subs.:* Martin, Lowry.
Referee: Mr. F. Desplas (Toulouse, France)
Attendance: 30,786.

WORLD EVENTS

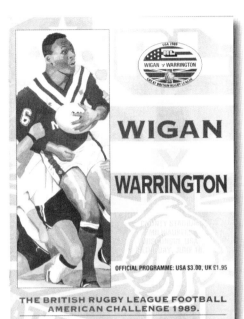

(*Above*) The programme from the American Challenge match in Milwaukee, Wisconsin in 1989, Wigan versus Warrington.

(*Above*) The French 50th anniversary celebration match in Paris in 1984, and the Oceania team who beat Europe comfortably.

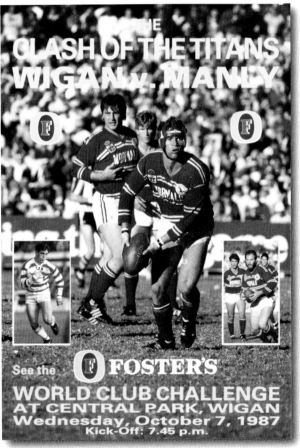

(*Above*) Mark Graham as captain of the 'Rest of the World' team against Australia in July 1988.

(*Above*) The memorable poster used to promote the famous Wigan versus Manly match in 1987.

NEW CLUBS EXPLOSION

(Above) The Fulham team, newly promoted, pictured at Craven Cottage before the start of their second season 1981-82. Left to right: *(Standing):* Harry Beverley, Martin Herdman, Joe Doherty, David Hull, John Wood, Roy Lester, Tony Gourley, Dave Allen, Neil Tuffs, Peter Souto. *(Seated):* Tony Kinsey, Steve Diamond, Derek Noonan, Carl Radbone, Reg Bowden, David Eckersley, Mal Aspey, Adrian Cambriani, John Crossley, Chris Ganley and John Dalgreen. The mascot at the front is young Christie Welland.

(Above)
Reg Bowden in action as player-coach for Fulham. Reg was a key signing for the new London club in 1980 and his presence helped recruit many more experienced players from Widnes and other northern clubs.

Rugby League saw an explosion of new professional clubs during the 1980s, which started in spectacular style when Fulham Football Club set up their own team just in time for the 1980-81 season. Fulham's Yorkshire born chairman Ernie Clay saw staging Rugby League at the picturesque Craven Cottage ground as a way of generating more 'brass' to prop up his struggling soccer team and, in their first season, it worked quite brilliantly. The Rugby League game had never enjoyed such positive publicity in the capital city as Fulham, with a team of experienced players who would train in the north and travel down to London on the weekends of their home matches, took the game by storm. Led by their tenacious player-coach Reg Bowden, Fulham kicked off with a memorable win over Wigan in front of nearly 10,000 people at Craven Cottage. They went on to win promotion at their first attempt and finished the season with an average crowd of 6,096, the fourth highest in the whole of the Rugby League. Fulham's instant success prompted numerous other Football League clubs to consider following their example, with two eventually

(Above) **New clubs in opposition as Ian Van Bellen, in Kent Invicta's debut match, tackles Cardiff City's Tommy David. The mighty Van Bellen was a real star of Fulham's first season which prompted Kent Invicta to recruit him.**

(Left)
The new Carlisle team pictured at Brunton Park before their debut in 1981. Left to right: *(Standing):* **Wally Youngman, Graham Evans, Nigel Stephenson, Terry Hollingsworth, Kevan Robinson, Tom Gainford, Jimmy Thompson, Steve Raybould, Graeme Robinson, Barry Limb.** *(Seated):* **Joe Bardgett, Steve Ferres, Allan Agar (player-coach), Dennis Boyd (capt.), Mick Morgan, Ian Crowther and Steve Davies.**

going ahead as Cardiff City and Carlisle United launched Rugby League teams in the 1981-82 season. Both followed the Fulham example of signing a team of travelling experienced players, although Cardiff - nicknamed the 'Blue Dragons' - also spent a lot of money in enticing well known Welsh Rugby Union players to join them. Carlisle, with Allan Agar as player-coach, were just as successful as Fulham in gaining promotion in their first season and attracting a very enthusiastic band of supporters in a new area for the game.

Sadly, after all their initial optimism, things turned sour for Fulham, Cardiff and Carlisle and their soccer landlords lost interest once Rugby League teams became a drain on finances rather than a profit maker. Fulham and Carlise eventually were run by enthusiasts and managed to re-establish themselves and stay alive throughout the decade, but Cardiff left Ninian Park to become Bridgend, and eventually dropped out of the Rugby League after the 1984-85 season. They were joined in their exit by Southend Invicta who had begun life as Kent Invicta in 1983 playing at Maidstone. Despite establishing a good base in Kent, Invicta's ill-fated move to Southend after one season was destined to fail, and it did. That was not before two more new clubs were admitted to the League in 1984, at Sheffield and Mansfield, which brought the total clubs in membership for 1984-85 to 36, the most since 1902-03. Mansfield Marksman were, intitially, based at the local football ground, but Sheffield Eagles were totally independent of football ties and overcame a low budget start to become established and go on to greater things.

(Above) **Gordon Pritchard in action for Cardiff Blue Dragons against Doncaster.** *(Right)* **A poster on the wall at Central Park in August 1984 advertising the arrival of Mansfield Marksman.**

CLUBS WHO CAME AND WENT IN THE '80s

Hello	*Goodbye*
Fulham	Cardiff City
Cardiff City	Huyton
Carlisle	Kent Invicta
Kent Invicta	Bridgend
Mansfield Marksman	Southend Invicta
Sheffield Eagles	Blackpool Borough
Bridgend	Springfield Borough
Runcorn Highfield	Chorley Borough
Southend Invicta	Mansfield Marksman
Springfield Borough	York
Chorley Borough	*(Clubs which disappeared were:*
Chorley	*Cardiff City, Bridgend, Kent*
Trafford Borough	*Invicta and Southend Invicta.*
Nottingham City	*All the others carried on under*
Ryedale York	*one name or another.)*

(Above) Fulham play Carlisle pre-season in London in 1981, with Mick Morgan and Roy Lester in the action.

NEW CLUBS

A look at how the new clubs of the 1980s brightened up Rugby League with their colourful programmes.

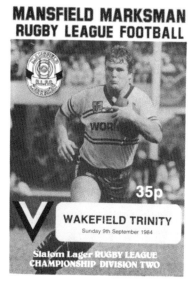

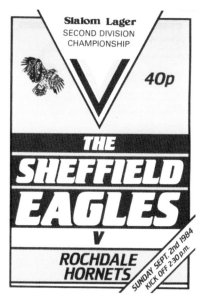

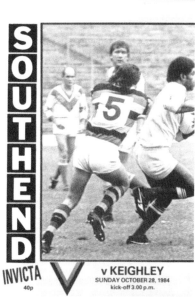

CLUB COLOURS

Bob Eccles, a top player throughout the '80s *(above)* packing down for Springfield Borough versus Leeds in 1987 and *(right)* in more familiar colours for Warrington being tackled by Oldham's Alan McCurrie.

(Above) The early days of Ellery Hanley in the classical colours of Bradford Northern.

(Clockwise) David Heron and Kevin Dick, two stars for Leeds; Rob Ackerman, the ex-Wales Rugby Union international, in action for Whitehaven against York; Paul Groves, the St.Helens hooker, reaches out to score against Swinton; Des Drummond of Leigh tackled by Warrington's Phil Ford.

COUNTY RUGBY LEAGUE

(Above) **Yorkshire coach Peter Fox holds the Rodstock War of the Roses trophy after his team's 24-14 victory over Lancashire in the 1988 match at Headingley. Yorkshire captain Ellery Hanley stands next to the coach.**

COUNTY CHAMPIONSHIP

1980-81
3rd September 1980 - at Barrow.
CUMBRIA 19, LANCASHIRE 16.
17th September 1980 - at Hull K.R.
YORKSHIRE 16, CUMBRIA 17.
24th September 1980 - at Widnes.
LANCASHIRE 17, YORKSHIRE 9.
Champions: CUMBRIA

1981-82
9th September 1981 - at Castleford.
YORKSHIRE 21, LANCASHIRE 15.
16th September 1981 - at Wigan.
LANCASHIRE 15, CUMBRIA 27.
23rd September 1981 - at Whitehaven.
CUMBRIA 20, YORKSHIRE 10.
Champions: CUMBRIA.

1982-83
23rd May 1982 - at Castleford.
YORKSHIRE 22, CUMBRIA 7.
26th May 1982 - at Leigh.
LANCASHIRE 21, YORKSHIRE 22.
30th May 1982 - at Workington.
CUMBRIA 8, LANCASHIRE 46.
Champions: YORKSHIRE

County Rugby League saw major changes in the 1980s, most fundamentally the abandonment of the County Championship in 1982 after 87 years. The old competition was cut by the Rugby League in most unsatisfactory fashion after they had brought forward the 1982-83 tournament to shortly after the end of the previous season, with all three games played in the last week of May 1982. Not surprisingly, there was little interest from either players or supporters at that time of year with the season effectively over, and those among the game's heirachy who wanted to get rid of the County Championship had their long awaited excuse.

It was a particularly damaging decision for the game in Cumbria, where the chance to compete in the County Championship was always regarded as a major incentive for their players and a galvanising promotional opportunity for the game. And the Cumbrians felt even more isolated and unwanted when, just three years later, the Rugby League set about building a new, high profile, event for the county game, but involving only Lancashire and Yorkshire. In an attempt to ape Australia's successful 'State of Origin' series between Queenland and New South Wales, the British Rugby League set up their own 'War of the Roses' - to be played under the banner of sponsors Rodstock, and promoted by the RFL as a major representative fixture rather than be left under the auspices of the old Lancashire and Yorkshire county committees (as had always been the case previously for county matches).

(Left)
Inside the Cumbrian dressing-room before their victory over Yorkshire on 23rd September 1981, which clinched their second successive title in the County Championship - this followed Cumbria's excellent win over Lancashire at Wigan seven days earlier. The picture shows Cumbrian captain Arnold Walker being massaged by his team-mates Alan McCurrie and Joe Stewart, whilst others looking on are (left to right): Lyn Hopkins, David Beck, Johnny Jones, Ralph McConnell, Mel Mason, Malcolm Flynn, Bobby Blackwood, Peter Gorley and Peter Stoddart.

The RFL also appointed high profile coaches Alex Muphy and Peter Fox for Lancashire and Yorkshire in an attempt to spice up the new 'War of the Roses', and Fox proved to be a major influence behind the white rose's successful domination of the series. On the other side of the Pennines, Murphy was eventually replaced as coach by Doug Laughton, but still success proved elusive for the Lancashire side. Staged alternately at the prestigious Test match grounds of Central Park and Headingley, the 'War of the Roses' was launched in 1985 and, immediately, the attendance was much bigger than the previous small crowds which had bothered with the County Championship in its latter years. Those crowds continued to grow throughout the 1980s, and certainly the Yorkshire players took great pride in turning out for their county and their coach, Peter Fox - a spirit perfectly illustrated when Ellery Hanley, returning from a high profile stint in Australia in 1988, virtually stepped straight off the plane to lead Yorkshire to their fourth consecutive win in a hard fought match at Headingley. The prestige of the 'War of the Roses' took a blow the following year, when Lancashire conceded 56 points on home turf.

Before the abandonment of the County Championship, Cumbria had enjoyed two successive title wins at the start of the decade - their first under the banner of Cumbria (rather than the original Cumberland) which had been created in 1973. The very last County Championship title was won by Yorkshire, which the record books show was (in theory) for the 1982-83 season. After that, Cumbria became dependent on the visit of touring teams to get a fixture which they did with every Kiwi and Kangaroo team throughout the decade, achieving a memorable 9-3 win over the New Zealanders in 1980 - and they also enjoyed a 16-all draw with the Great Britain team (coached by Maurice Bamford) in 1985; before beating both Papua New Guinea in 1987 and France in 1988.

WAR OF THE ROSES

1985
11th September 1985 - at Wigan.
LANCASHIRE 10, YORKSHIRE 26.
Attendance: 6,743.

1986
17th September 1986 - at Headingley.
YORKSHIRE 26, LANCASHIRE 14.
Attendance: 5,983.

1987
16th September 1987 - at Wigan.
LANCASHIRE 10, YORKSHIRE 16.
Attendance: 9,748.

1988
21st September 1988 - at Headingley.
YORKSHIRE 24, LANCASHIRE 14.
Attendance: 8,244.

1989
20th September 1989 - at Wigan.
LANCASHIRE 12, YORKSHIRE 56.
Attendance: 10,182.

FROM INVINCIBLES TO UNFORGETTABLES

Just four of the 1982 Kangaroo 'Invincibles' who came back to play in the colours of English clubs: *(clockwise)* Wally Lewis for Wakefield Trinity, Peter Sterling for Hull in the 1985 Cup Final, Eric Grothe for Leeds, and Brett Kenny of Wigan savouring the Wembley atmosphere after winning the 1985 Lance Todd trophy.

UNION INTERNATIONALS

(Above) A Scostman, a Welshman and an Englishman - three Rugby Union internationals who turned to League in the 1980s. From the left: Alan Tait (Widnes), Terry Holmes (Bradford) and John Bentley (Leeds).

R ugby League's commercial vibrancy in the latter years of the 1980s saw a revival of that well worn path from South Wales to the north of England for numerous Welsh Rugby Union players, among them several very high profile internationals. But, before then, the formation of the Cardiff City 'Blue Dragons' in 1981 provided a lucrative pay-day towards the end of their playing careers for three of Welsh Union's favourite sons, Steve Fenwick, Tommy David and Paul Ringer. They were followed by Brynmor Williams, and all enjoyed the luxury of cashing in on Rugby League's professionalism without having to leave their homes in South Wales. That no longer applied after the demise of the 'Blue Dragons' and other Welsh players faced the usual move to the north - among them two of the highest profile signings of all time in Terry Holmes and Jonathan Davies. Holmes was restricted by injuries from his unhappy debut for Bradford away at Swinton, but Davies - eased into the game more gently by Widnes - developed into an outstanding Rugby League player. Despite the lengthy list *(below)* some of the very best converts from Rugby Union in the '80s were not full internationals, among them Martin Offiah, Mark Preston and Hugh Waddell.

(Above) Ex-Wales and British Lions centre Rob Ackerman scores a try for Whitehaven versus Fulham.

UNION INTERNATIONALS SIGNED BY BRITISH RUGBY LEAGUE CLUBS

Wales
Tommy David *(Pontypridd)* -Cardiff City, 1981-82.
Steve Fenwick *(Bridgend)* -Cardiff City, 1981-82
Paul Ringer *(Llanelli)* -Cardiff City, 1981-82
Brynmor Williams *(Swansea)* -Cardiff City, 1982-83
Terry Holmes *(Cardiff)* -Bradford Northern, 1985-86
Rob Ackerman *(Cardiff)* -Whitehaven, 1985-86
Gary Pearce *(Llanelli)* -Hull F.C., 1986-87
Stuart Evans *(Neath)* -St.Helens, 1987-88
Adrian Hadley *(Cardiff)* -Salford, 1988-89
David Bishop *(Pontypool)* -Hull K.R., 1988-89
Jonathan Griffiths *(Llanelli)* -St.Helens, 1988-89

Jonathan Davies *(Llanelli)* -Widnes, 1988-89
Paul Moriarty *(Swansea)* -Widnes, 1988-89
John Devereux *(Bridgend)* -Widnes, 1989-90

England
Steve Redfearn *(Leicester Tigers)* -Sheffield, 1984-85
Peter Williams *(Orrell)* -Salford, 1987-88
John Bentley *(Sale)* -Leeds, 1988-89

Scotland
Alan Tait *(Kelso)* -Widnes, 1987-88

New Zealand
Mark Brooke-Cowden *(Auckland)* -Leeds, 1987-88

CHALLENGE CUP FINALS

(Pictured) Joe Lydon celebrates his Lance Todd Trophy winning display at Wembley in the 1984 Challenge Cup Final with his Widnes colleagues. They had just beaten Wigan to win the Cup.

(Above)
The programme for the 1980 Cup Final, when both the Hull clubs helped pack Wembley to the rafters. Note the sponsorship of State Express had arrived.

Wembley saw some magical moments during the 1980s as the Rugby League Challenge Cup Final reached new peaks, both in the colour and excitement of the game on the lush turf and the commericial juggernaut it became for the Rugby Football League off the pitch. The decade began with an unprecedented Hull derby under the twin towers, which also marked the long awaited first Wembley appearance for Roger Millward. We also saw the finah hurrah for the outstanding Widnes side which had come to regard Wembley as almost a second home during the latter part of the 1970s. There was also a Challenge Cup Final replay for the first time since Odsal in 1954, and with that came a night of wonderful drama under the floodlights of Elland Road in Leeds, pointing the way ahead to the use of large football stadiums for the staging of major Rugby League games. There was no shortage of fairytale romance as Featherstone Rovers, with a team of local boys, beat big-spending Hull in 1983, Castleford repeated the dose against the other Humberside giants of Hull K.R., to be followed a year later by Halifax, back at Wembley for the first time in over 30 years. And by the end of the decade the foundations of the incredible Wigan dynasty that was to come had already been laid. And the icing on the cake was the epic Cup Final of 1985, which was a landmark moment for the game. An official capacity crowd of almost 98,000 was given that day, but suggestions were it was actually well over 100,000. The first million pound 'gate' came in 1987, before the 'all-seater' revamp of Wembley Stadium saw capacity reduced to 78,000 from 1989 onwards.

(Right) Both clubs from the city of Hull would become no strangers to Wembley during the 1980s, after the decade had begun with the unique occasion of Hull Kingston Rovers and Hull F.C. meeting each other under the twin towers. The Robins came out on top, 10-5, but it was very close as *(above)* referee Fred Lindop disallows Hull's claim for a try, leading to Cup winning delight at last for Rovers' Roger Millward.

CHALLENGE CUP FINALS IN THE '80s

1980

Saturday 3rd May 1980, at Wembley Stadium

Hull Kingston Rovers 10, Hull 5.

Hull K.R. Try: Hubbard..
Goals: Hubbard (3). Drop-goal: Millward.
Hull: Try: Wilby. Goal: Lloyd.
HULL K.R.: D.Hall; S.Hubbard, M.Smith, S.Hartley, C.Sullivan; R.Millward, A.Agar; R.Holdstock, D.Watkinson, B.Lockwood, P.Rose, P.Lowe, L.Casey. *Subs.:* P.Hogan (for Hubbard), J.Millington (for Rose).
HULL: P.Woods; G.Bray, G.Walters, T.Wilby, P.Prendiville; J.Newlove, C.Pickerill; K.Tindall, R.Wileman, R.Stone, C.Birdsall, G.Lloyd, S.Norton. *Subs.:* B.Hancock (for Newlove), V.Farrar (for Stone).
Referee: Mr. G.F. Lindop (Wakefield)
Attendance: 95,000. (capacity). Receipts: £448,202.

1981

Saturday 2nd May 1981, at Wembley Stadium

Widnes 18, Hull Kingston Rovers 9.

Widnes: Tries: Burke, George, Gregory.
Goals: Burke (4). Drop-goal: Adams.
Hull K.R.: Try: Burton. Goals: Hubbard (3).
WIDNES: M.Burke; S.Wright, M.George, E.Cunningham, K.Bentley; E.Hughes, A.Gregory; M.O'Neill, K.Elwell, B.Lockwood, L.Gorley, E.Prescott, M.Adams. *Subs.:* J.Myler (for Cunningham), G.Shaw (for O'Neill).
HULL K.R.: D.Hall; S.Hubbard, M.Smith, P.Hogan, P.Muscroft; S.Hartley, P.Harkin; R.Holdstock, D.Watkinson, S.Crooks, P.Lowe, C.Burton, L.Casey. *Subs.:* P.Proctor (for Crooks), J.Millington (for Holdstock).
Referee: Mr. G. Kershaw (Easingwold)
Attendance: 92,496. Receipts: £591,117.

1982

Saturday 1st May 1982, at Wembley Stadium

Hull 14, Widnes 14.

Hull: Tries: Norton, O'Hara. Goals: Lloyd (4).
Widnes: Tries: Cunningham (2), Wright.
Goals: Burke, Gregory. Drop-goal: Elwell.
HULL: G.Kemble; D.O'Hara, T.Day, S.Evans, P.Prendiville; D.Topliss, K.Harkin; T.Skerrett, R.Wileman, R.Stone, M.Crane, G.Lloyd, S.Norton. *Subs.:* L.Crooks (for Crane).
WIDNES: M.Burke; S.Wright, K.O'Loughlin, E.Cunningham, J.Basnett; E.Hughes, A.Gregory; M.O'Neill, K.Elwell, B.Lockwood, L.Gorley, E.Prescott, M.Adams. *Subs.:* T.Myler (for Burke), S.O'Neill (for Lockwood).
Referee: Mr. G.F. Lindop (Wakefield).
Attendance: 92,147. Receipts: £684,500.

1982 - Replay

Wednesday 19th May 1982, at Elland Road, Leeds.

Hull 18, Widnes 9.

Hull: Tries: Topliss (2), Kemble, Crooks.
Goals: Crooks (3).
Widnes: Try: Wright. Goals: Burke (3).
HULL: G.Kemble; C.Sullivan, J.Leuluai, S.Evans, P.Prendiville; D.Topliss, T.Dean; K.Tindall, T.Duke, R.Stone, T.Skerrett, L.Crooks, S.Norton. *Subs.:* M.Crane (for Norton).
WIDNES: M.Burke: S.Wright, K.O'Loughlin, E.Cunningham, J.Basnett; E.Hughes, A.Gregory; M.O'Neill, K.Elwell, B.Lockwood, L.Gorley, E.Prescott, M.Adams. *Subs.:*
Referee: Mr. G.F. Lindop (Wakefield)
Attendance: 41,171. Receipts: £180,525.

The emotions of winning the Challenge Cup. *(Above, left)* Joy for Featherstone Rovers David Hobbs and Ken Kellett after their win at Wembley in 1983. *(Middle)* Hull F.C. coach Arthur Bunting is elated as the final whistle blows in the 1982 Cup Final replay at Elland Road and his team have beaten Widnes. *(Right)* The iconic image of the wonderful 1985 Wembley Final, as Wigan's Brett Kenny and Hull's Peter Sterling, team-mates and friends at home in Australia, come face to face after Wigan's 28-24 victory.

1983

Saturday 7th May 1983, at Wembley Stadium.

Featherstone Rovers 14, Hull 12.

Featherstone: Tries: Hobbs (2). Goals: Quinn (4).
Hull: Tries: Leuluai, Crooks. Goals: Crooks (3).
FEATHERSTONE: N.Barker; J,Marsden, S.Quinn, J.Gilbert, K.Kellett; A.Banks, T.Hudson; M.Gibbins, R.Handscombe, S.Hankins, D.Hobbs, T.Slatter, P.Smith.
Subs.: P.Lyman (for Gilbert), G.Siddall (for Slatter)
HULL: G.Kemble; D.O'Hara, S.Evans, J.Leuluai, P.Prendiville; D.Topliss, K.Harkin; T.Skerrett, J.Bridges, R.Stone, P.Rose, L.Crooks, S.Norton.
Subs.: T.Day (for Harkin), M.Crane (for Day).
Referee: Mr. R. Whitfield (Widnes).
Attendance: 84,475. Receipts: £655,510.

1984

Saturday 5th May 1984, at Wembley Stadium.

Widnes 19, Wigan 6.

Widnes: Tries: Lydon (2), O'Loughlin.
Goals: Burke (3). Drop-goal: S.O'Neill.
Wigan: Try: Helmsley. Goal: Whitfield.
WIDNES: M.Burke; S.Wright, E.Hughes, J.Lydon, J.Basnett; K.O'Loughlin, A.Gregory; S.O'Neill, K.Elwell, K.Tamati, L.Gorley, M.O'Neill, M.Adams.
Subs.: D.Hulme (for Hughes), F.Whitfield (for M.O'Neill).
WIGAN: S.Edwards; D.Ramsdale, D.Stephenson, C.Whitfield, H.Gill; M.Cannon, G.Stephens; K.Hemsley, H.Tamati, B.Case, G.West, M.Scott, J.Pendlebury. *Subs.:* W.Elvin (for Whitfield), B.Juliff (for Case).
Referee: Mr. W.H. Thompson (Huddersfield).
Attendance: 80,116. Receipts: £686,171.

(Above) **Contrasting moods for Vince Karalius and Alex Murphy on the coaches' bench in 1984.**

1985

Saturday 4th May 1985, at Wembley Stadium.

Wigan 28, Hull 24.

Wigan: Tries: Ferguson (2),Gill, Kenny, Edwards.
Goals: Gill (3), Stephenson.
Hull: Tries: Leuluai (2), James, Evans, Divorty.
Goals: Crooks (2).
WIGAN: S. Edwards; J.Ferguson, D.Stephenson, S.Donlan, H.Gill; B.Kenny, M.Ford; N.Courtney, N.Kiss, B.Case, G.West, B.Dunn, I.Potter.
Subs.: D.Campbell (for Case), N.du Toit (not used).
HULL; G.Kemble; K.James, S.Evans, J.Leuluai, D.O'Hara; F.Ah Kuoi, P.Sterling; L.Crooks, S.Patrick, N.Puckering, J.Muggleton, P.Rose, S.Norton.
Subs.: G.Schofield (for O'Hara), G.Divorty (for Puckering).
Referee: Mr. R. Campbell (Widnes).
Attendance: 97,801. (capacity). Receipts: £760,322..

(Above) The crucial tackle by loose-forward John Pendlebury in the closing minutes of the 1987 Wembley Final which saved the Cup for Halifax. Pendlebury managed to knock the ball out of the hands of the St.Helens centre Mark Elia as he crossed the line, and Halifax hung on to win 19-18, Pendlebury's drop-goal proving to be the one point margin of victory. *(Right)* The Castleford scrum-half Bob Beardmore shows his winner's medal after his Lance Todd Trophy winning display in the 1986 Final when Cas' beat Hull K.R. 15-14.

1986

Saturday 3rd May 1986, at Wembley Stadium.

Castleford 15, Hull Kingston Rovers 14.

Castleford: Tries: Marchant, Sandy, R.Beardmore.
*Goals: R.Beardmore, Ketteridge. **Drop-goal:** R.Beardmore.*
Hull K.R.: Tries: Prohm (2), Lydiat. Goal: Dorahy.
CASTLEFORD: .G.Lord; D.Plange, T.Marchant, G.Hyde, J.Sandy; J.Joyner, R.Beardmore; K.Ward, K.Beardmore, B.Johnson, K.England, M.Ketteridge, I.French.
Subs.: D.Rookley (for Lord), S.Horton (for K.Beardmore).
HULL K.R.: G.Fairbairn; G.Clark, M.Smith, G.Prohm, D.Laws; J.Dorahy, P.Harkin; P.Johnston, D.Watkinson, A.Ema, A.Kelly, D.Harrison, G.Miller.
Subs.: G.Smith (for Kelly), J.Lydiat (for Harrison)
Referee: Mr. R. Whitfield (Widnes).
Attendance: 82,134.. Receipts: £806,676.

1987

Saturday 2nd May 1987, at Wembley Stadium.

Halifax 19, St.Helens 18.

Halifax: Tries: George, McCallion, Eadie.
*Goals: Whitfield (3). **Drop-goal:** Pendlebury.*
St.Helens: Tries: Loughlin, Round, Elia. Goals: Loughlin (3).
HALIFAX: G.Eadie; S.Wilson, C.Whitfield, G.Rix, W.George; C.Anderson, G.Stephens; G.Beevers, S.McCallion, K.Neller, P.Dixon, M.Scott, J.Pendlebury.
Subs.: B.Juliff (for Anderson), N.James (for Beevers).
ST.HELENS: P.Veivers; B.Ledger, P.Loughlin, M.Elia, K.McCormack; B.Clark, N.Holding; T.Burke, G.Liptrot, J.Fieldhouse, A.Platt, R.Haggerty, C.Arkwright. *Subs.: P.Round (for Haggerty), P.Forber.*
Referee: Mr. J. Holdsworth (Kippax).
Attendance: 91,267. Receipts: £1,009,206.

1988

Saturday 30th April 1988, at Wembley Stadium.

Wigan 32, Halifax 12.

Wigan: Tries: K.Iro (2), Lydon, Bell, Gill, T.Iro, Hanley.
Goals: Lydon, Gregory.
Halifax: Tries: Anderson, James.
Goals: Whitfield (2).
WIGAN: J.Lydon; T.Iro, K.Iro, D.Bell, H.Gill; S.Edwards, A.Gregory; B.Case, N.Kiss, A.Shelford, A.Goodway, I.Potter, E.Hanley.
Subs.: G.Byrne (for Edwards), S.Wane (for Potter).
HALIFAX: G.Eadie; M.Meredith, T.Anderson, I.Wilkinson, C.Whitfield; B.Grogan, S.Robinson; N.James, S.McCallion, K.Neller, L.Holliday, P.Dixon, J.Pendlebury. *Subs.: M.Scott (for Holliday), D.Fairbank (for Robinson).*
Referee: Mr. G.F. Lindop (Wakefield).
Attendance: 94,273. Receipts: £1,102,247.

1989

Saturday 29th April 1989, at Wembley Stadium.

Wigan 27, St.Helens 0.

Wigan: Tries: K.Iro (2), Gregory, Hanley, Hampson.
*Goals: Lydon (3). **Drop-goal:** Gregory.*
WIGAN: S.Hampson; T.Iro, K.Iro, D.Bell, J.Lydon; S.Edwards, A.Gregory; I.Lucas, N.Kiss, A.Shelford, A,Platt, I.Potter, E.Hanley. *Subs.: A.Goodway (for Potter), D.Betts (for Kiss).*
ST.HELENS: G.Connolly; M.O'Connor, P.Veivers, P.Loughlin, L.Quirk; S.Cooper, N.Holding; T.Burke, P.Groves, P.Forber, B.Dwyer, R.Haggerty, P.Vautin.
Subs.: D.Bloor (for Loughlin), S.Evans (for Dwyer).
Referee: Mr. R. Tennant (Castleford).
Attendance: 78,000 (capacity). Receipts: £1,121,293.

CHAMPIONSHIP WINNERS

(Above) A trio of Championship winning captains who led from the front - *from the left:* Kurt Sorensen of Widnes in 1989; Chris Anderson of Halifax in 1986; and Len Casey of Hull Kingston Rovers in 1984.

(Above) John Woods - led Leigh to the Championship in the 1981-82 season.

Championship Winners

1979-80	Bradford Northern
1980-81	Bradford Northern
1981-82	Leigh
1982-83	Hull
1983-84	Hull Kingston Rovers
1984-85	Hull Kingston Rovers
1985-86	Halifax
1986-87	Wigan
1987-88	Widnes
1988-89	Widnes

Since the introduction of two divisions in 1973, the profile given to the Championship winners in Rugby League struggled to match that of the Challenge Cup winners. With the champions decided on a first-past-the-post basis, they no longer had the high profile stage of the Championship Final to claim their prize on - indeed, even the end of season Premiership Final winners got more publicity by virtue of that game being televised by the BBC. Yet for the game's purists, winning the Championship remained the ultimate accolade for any team as a tribute to their consistency and allround ability to survive a nine month campaign through a wide variety of conditions. The Rugby League Champions were the best of the best.

The RFL's public relations officer, David Howes, did his best to build the profile of the Championship during the 1980s by attracting sponsorship, first from Slalom Lager and then from 1986-87 onwards, Stones Bitter. The advent of television coverage from the ITV regions, Granada, Yorkshire and Border, also played a significant part in boosting the image of the competition, so that by the time Widnes were clinching the last title of the decade in 1989 they were able to do so in a televised thriller against Wigan. That had not been the case for some of their predecessors. Three clubs -Bradford Northern, Hull K.R. and Widnes - were able to achieve the admirable feat of winning back to back Championships, but throughout the 'eighties nobody managed to win a Cup and League 'double'. Hull probably thought they were going to do that in 1983, when they celebrated winning the Championship after victory over Barrow in their last league game of the season by treating the Boulevard crowd to a 'haka' in homage to their Kiwi trio of Kemble, Leuluai and O'Hara; only to be beaten at Wembley by Cup giant-killers Featherstone Rovers. There were no Championships in the 'eighties for two of the

(Above) **The Robins of Hull Kingston Rovers after being presented with the Championship trophy for the 1983-84 season at their home Craven Park. Captain Len Casey and prop John Millington flank the trophy and young mascot at the front; the players standing behind are, left to right: Phil Hogan, Mark Broadhurst, David Hall, George Fairbairn, Steve Hartley, Garry Clark, Steve Dobson, John Dorahy, Paul Proctor, Chris Rudd, David Laws, Andy Kelly, John Lydiat, Gary Prohm, Chris Burton, Gordon Smith and Mike Smith.**

game's most powerful clubs, St.Helens and Leeds; and when Wigan broke their duck in 1987 it was the first time the Championship trophy had been brought back to Central Park since 1960. There were two romantic 'under dog' tales during the decade as both Leigh, in 1982, then Halifax, in 1986, surprised the established powers in the game by winning the Championship. Both titles came with plenty of last minute drama, as Halifax endured a 13-all draw against Featherstone in their last match to get the point they needed in '86, and Leigh, four years earlier, journeyed with an army of fans for a midweek decider at faraway Whitehaven. Down at half-time, those Leigh fans were on a knife-edge before a second-half try by Des Drummond turned the game and the title.

(Above) **Wigan celebrate winning the Championship in 1987 - the club's first title for 27 years and a real feather in the cap of their new coach Graham Lowe.**

(Left) **Bradford Northern, Champions in 1981 for the second successive year. Left to right: *(Standing):* David Redfearn, Phil Sanderson, Graham Idle, Alan Redfearn, Jeff Grayshon, Phil Jackson, Keith Mumby. *(In front):* Alan Parker, David Barends, Jimmy Thompson, Nigel Stephenson, Tony Handforth and Derek Parker.**

SECOND DIVISION CHAMPIONS

(Above) York were Champions of the Second Division in 1981, and the Wasps' winning team is pictured here at Clarence Street, with their captain Kevin Harkin holding the prized rosebowl trophy and coach Bill Kirkbride standing on the far right of the middle row. Other players include: Paul McDermott, Peter Roe, Gary Price, Derek Foster, Alan Wardell, Geoff Pryce and Brendan White.

Second Division Champions

1979-80	Featherstone
1980-81	York
1981-82	Oldham
1982-83	Fulham
1983-84	Barrow
1984-85	Swinton
1985-86	Leigh
1986-87	Hunslet
1987-88	Oldham
1988-89	Leigh

The so called 'yo-yo syndrome' between Rugby League's two divisions did nothing to stop the ambition of clubs trying to win promotion, and attendance figures in the 1980s clearly showed the public's appetite for winning teams aiming to go up. After Featherstone Rovers started the decade by being promoted as Second Division leaders (and remember Rovers were the Rugby League Champions just three years earlier in 1977) the arrival of Fulham did much to boost the profile of Division Two - not just in London but across the north of England where every other club wanted to beat them. Fulham won promotion in their debut season, 1980-81, as York were crowned champions and Wigan got the immediate return to the top flight they so desperately needed. Twelve months later, Reg Bowden's boys experienced the other side of the coin (or, indeed, the yo-yo) as they were narrowly relegated, but then bounced back as Second Division champions in their third season. Remarkably, all four teams who were promoted in 1983 (Fulham, Salford, Wakefield and Whitehaven) came down

(Left) Barrow players enjoy a lap of honour at Craven Park after being presented with the Second Division Championship trophy for 1983-84. Captain Alan Hodkinson is holding both the trophy and a £7,000 cheque from sponsors, Slalom Lager. It climaxed a fine season for Barrow in which they also won the Lancashire Cup.

again the following year in exactly the same positions - yet the gap between the two divisions was not that wide as promoted teams battled strongly and several Second Division sides did well in Cup competitions, notably Barrow in winning the Lancashire Cup in 1983 and York going very close to Wembley in '84. Barrow rode the 'yo-yo' more than any other club in the 'eighties, going down and up in five consecutives years between 1983 and '87, before going up again in 1989. Halifax showed it was possible to bridge the gap rapidly, becoming Rugby League Champions just two years after being promoted (from fourth place) in 1984. Going in the opposite direction, Leigh won the Championship title in 1982 and three years later were relegated to the Second Division. Some clubs were unlucky when the number of promotion places was reduced to three, and only two in 1987 to accomodate a decrease in the number of clubs in the First Division from 16 to 14, in the year when Hunslet and Swinton went up and met in the first Old Trafford Premiership Final.

(Above) Whitehaven scrum-half Arnold Walker was a key to their winning promotion in 1980-81.

UPS AND DOWNS, PROMOTION AND RELEGATION IN THE 80s

1979-80
Promoted:
Featherstone
Halifax
Oldham
Barrow
Relegated:
Wigan
Hunslet
York
Blackpool

1980-81
Promoted:
York
Wigan
Fulham
Whitehaven
Relegated:
Halifax
Salford
Workington
Oldham

1981-82
Promoted:
Oldham
Carlisle
Workington
Halifax
Relegated:
Fulham
Wakefield
York
Whitehaven

1982-83
Promoted:
Fulham
Wakefield
Salford
Whitehaven
Relegated:
Barrow
Workington
Halifax
Carlisle

1983-84
Promoted:
Barrow
Workington
Hunslet
Halifax
Relegated:
Fulham
Wakefield
Salford
Whitehaven

1984-85
Promoted:
Swinton
Salford
York
Dewsbury
Relegated:
Barrow
Leigh
Hunslet
Workington

1985-86
Promoted:
Leigh
Barrow
Wakefield
Relgated:
York
Swinton
Dewsbury

1986-87*
Promoted:
Hunslet
Swinton
Relegated:
Oldham
Featherstone
Barrow
Wakefield
(* Ony two pro-
moted as size of
Division One
reduced to 14).

1987-88
Promoted:
Oldham
Featherstone
Wakefield
Relegated:
Leigh
Salford
Hunslet

1988-89
Promoted:
Leigh
Barrow
Sheffield E.
Relegated:
Oldham
Halifax
Hull K.R.

(Pictured at top)
Leigh captain
Alan Platt -
1989 winners.

PREMIERSHIP FINALS

One for the Wire

(*Above*) **Captain Les Boyd lifts the Premiership Trophy after Warrington's win over Halifax in 1986.**

Nothing emphasised the rising profile and morale in British Rugby League as the 1980s progressed better than the status of the Premiership Final. The tournament introduced largely to provide a second end of season Final to replace the old Championship Finals enjoyed before the introduction of two divisions, began the decade with a crowd of

PREMIERSHIP FINALS IN THE ·80s

1980

Saturday 17th May 1980, at Station Road, Swinton
Widnes 19, Bradford Northern 5.
Widnes: Tries: Wright, Aspey, Bentley, Elwell, Gorley.
Goal: Burke. Drop-goals: Eckersley, Elwell.
Bradford: Try: David Redfearn. Goal: Mumby.
WIDNES: M.Burke; S.Wright, M.George, M.Aspey, K.Bentley; D.Eckersley, R.Bowden; G.Shaw, K.Elwell, M.O'Neill, L.Gorley, D.Hull, M.Adams.
Subs.: David Moran (not used), B.Hogan (for Hull).
BRADFORD NORTHERN: K.Mumby; I.MacLean, David Redfearn, D.Parker, L.Gant; N.Stephenson, Alan Redfearn; J.Thompson, J.Bridges, C.Forsyth, G.Clarkson, J.Grayshon, G.Hale. *Subs.:* S.Ferres (for MacLean), G.Van Bellen (for Clarkson).
Referee: Mr. W. H. Thompson (Huddersfield)
Attendance: 10,215. Receipts: £13,665.

1981

Saturday 16th May 1981, at Headingley, Leeds
Hull Kingston Rovers 11, Hull 7.
Hull K.R.: Tries: Hartley, Hogan, Smith.
Goal: Hubbard.
Hull: Try: Crane.
Goals: Woods (2).
HULL KINGSTON ROVERS: P.Proctor; S.Hubbard, M.Smith, P.Hogan, P.Muscroft; S.Hartley, P.Harkin; R.Holdstock, D.Watkinson, J.Millington, P.Lowe, L.Casey, D.Hall. *Subs.:* C.Burton (for Hall).
HULL: P.Woods; G.Peacham, D.Elliott, T.Wilby, P.Prendiville; B.Banks, T.Dean; K.Tindall, R.Wileman, R.Stone, T.Skerrett, M.Crane, S.Norton
Subs.: I.Madley (for Skerrett).
Referee: Mr. J. Holdsworth (Kippax)
Attendance: 29,448. Receipts: 47,529.

just over 10,000 providing receipts of £13,665 at Swinton - and ended it just a few miles across Manchester with a crowd in excess of 40,000 and a staggering increase in receipts of £264,242. Sponsorship was also a key part of the Premiership as it created a high-profile big event to be broadcast live on television. Those sponsors were, for the first seven years of the decade, Slalom Lager, and from 1987 onwards Stone Bitter. 1987 also saw the relocating of the Premiership Final to Old Trafford, which proved to be the masterstroke in drawing hugely increased crowds and raising the wider profile of the event. Before that move to the home of Manchester United, the only comparable Premiership Final crowd came when almost 30,000 packed Headingley in 1981 for the clash between the two Hull clubs. On only four occasions during the 1980s did the Championship winners go on to win the Premiership Trophy, they were: Hull Kingston Rovers in 1984, Wigan in '87 and Widnes, who did it back to back, in 1988 and '89.

(*Above*) **Mick Adams of Widnes raises the Trophy in 1982 - the first of two successive Premiership Final wins over Hull for the Chemics.**

1982
Saturday 15th May, 1982, at Headingley, Leeds
Widnes 23, Hull 8.
Widnes: Tries: Basnett, Burke, Wright, Hughes, Adams.
Goals: Burke (4).
Hull: Try: Crooks.
Goals: Crooks (2). Drop-goal: Crooks.
WIDNES: M.Burke; S.Wright, K.O'Loughlin, E.Cunningham, J.Basnett; E.Hughes, A.Gregory; M.O'Neill, K.Elwell, B.Lockwood, L.Gorley, E.Prescott, M.Adams. *Subs.:* T.Myler (for Cunningham), F.Whitfield (for Lockwood).
HULL: G.Kemble; D.O'Hara, J.Leuluai, S.Evans, P.Prendiville; D.Topliss, K.Harkin; K.Tindall, R.Wileman, R.Stone, T.Skerrett, L.Crooks, S.Norton. *Subs,:* T.Day (for O'Hara), S.Lloyd (for Wileman).
Referee: Mr. S. Wall (Leigh)
Attendance: 12,100. Receipts: £23,749.

1983
Saturday 14th May, 1983, at Headingley Leeds
Widnes 22, Hull 10.
Widnes: Tries: Basnett (2), Myler, Gregory.
Goals: Lydon (5).
Hull: Tries: O'Hara, Topliss. Goals: Crooks (2).
WIDNES: M.Burke; R.Linton, E.Hughes, J.Lydon, J.Basnett; T.Myler, A.Gregory; M.O'Neill, K.Elwell, L.Gorley, F.Whitfield, E.Prescott, M.Adams. *Subs.:* D.Hulme (for Gregory), S.O'Neill for (Whitfield).
HULL: G.Kemble; D.O'Hara, T.Day, J.Leuluai, S.Evans; D.Topliss, T.Dean; T.Skerrett, J.Bridges, R.Stone, P.Rose, L.Crooks, S.Norton.
Subs.: P.Solal (for Day), M.Crane (for Norton).
Referee: Mr. F. Lindop (Wakefield)
Attendance: 17,813. Receipts: £34,145.

1984
Saturday 12th May, 1984, at Headingley, Leeds
Hull Kingston Rovers 18, Castleford 10.
Hull K.R.: Tries: Prohm, Smith, Laws, Dorahy.
Goal: Dorahy.
Castleford: Try: Kear. Goals: Beardmore (3).
HULL KINGSTON ROVERS: G.Fairbairn; G.Clark, M.Smith, G.Prohm, D.Laws; J.Dorahy, P.Harkin; R.Holdstock, C.Rudd, J.Millington, C.Burton, M.Broadhurst, D.Hall.
Subs.: I.Robinson (for Millington), J.Lydiat (for Burton).
CASTLEFORD: D.Roockley; D.Coen, T.Marchant, G.Hyde, J.Kear; S.Robinson, R.Beardmore; K.Ward, S.Horton, G.Connell, J.Crampton, B.Atkins, J.Joyner.
Subs.: I.Orum, D.Mountain (neither used).
Referee: Mr. R. Campbell (Widnes)
Attendance: 12,515. Receipts: £ 31,769.

1985
Saturday 11th May, 1985, at Elland Road, Leeds.
St.Helens 36, Hull Kingston Rovers 16.
St.Helens: Tries: Meninga (2), Ledger, Ainsworth, Veivers, Pinner. Goals: Day (4).
Hull K.R.: Tries: Fairbairn, Laws, Robinson.
Goals: Fairbairn (2).
ST.HELENS: P.Veivers; B.Ledger, S.Peters, M.Meninga, S.Day; C.Arkwright, N.Holding; T.Burke, G.Ainsworth, P.Gorley, A.Platt, R.Haggerty, H.Pinner.
Subs.: S.Allen (for Meninga), P.Forber (for Burke).
HULL KINGSTON ROVERS: G.Fairbairn; G.Clark, I.Robinson, G.Prohm, D.Laws; M.Smith, G.Smith; M.Broadhurst, D.Watkinson, A.Ema, A.Kelly, P.Hogan, D.Hall. *Subs.:* J.Lydiat (for Ema), P.Harkin (for G.Smith).
Referee: Mr. S. Wall (Leigh)
Attendance: 15,518. Receipts: £46,950.

(Above) **Hull K.R. captain David Hall receives the Premiership Trophy in 1984 from the RFL President, Lord Derby.**

No individual made a bigger impact on a Premiership Final than Mal Meninga, the mighty Australian centre who starred for St.Helens as they won the trophy in 1985, beating Hull K.R. at Elland Road. *(Above)* The Saints team celebrate as they carry skipper Harry Pinner shoulder high, with Meninga sharing their joy as he stands second from the right.

1986

Sunday 18th May, 1986 at Elland Road, Leeds
Warrington 38, Halifax 10.
Warrington: Tries: *Boyd (2), Bishop, Tamati, Jackson, Johnson, Forster.* **Goals:** *Bishop (5).*
Halifax: Try: *Chris Anderson.* **Goals:** *Whitfield (3).*
WARRINGTON: Paul Ford; M.Forster, P.Cullen, R.Duane, B.Carbert; P.Bishop, A.Gregory; L.Boyd, K.Tamati, R.Jackson, G.Sanderson, M.Roberts, M.Gregory.
Subs.: B.Johnson (for Ford), W.McGinty (for Sanderson).
HALIFAX: C.Whitfield; E.Riddlesden, T.Anderson, C.Anderson, S.Wilson; J.Crossley, G.Stephens; M.Scott, S.McCallion, G.Robinson, B.Juliff, N.James, P.Dixon.
Subs.: S.Smith (for Whitfield), S.Bond (for James).
Referee: Mr. F. Lindop (Wakefield)
Attendance: 13,683. **Receipts:** *£50,879.*

1987

Sunday 17th May, 1987 at Old Trafford, Manchester
Wigan 8, Warrington 0.
Wigan: Try: *Lydon.*
Goals: *Stephenson, Gill.*
WIGAN: S.Hampson, H.Gill, D.Stephenson, D.Bell, J.Lydon; S.Edwards, A.Gregory; B.Case, N.Kiss, S.Wane, A.Goodway, I.Potter, E.Hanley.
Subs.: R.Russell (for Lydon), G.West (for Wane).
WARRINGTON: B.Johnson, D.Drummond, J.Ropati, B.Peters, M.Forster; P.Cullen, P.Bishop; K.Tamati, M.Roberts, R.Jackson, A.Humphries, G.Sanderson, R.Duane. *Subs.:* M.Gregory (for Humphries), R.Eccles (for Roberts).
Referee: Mr. K. Allatt (Southport)
Attendance: 38,756. **Receipts:** *£165,166.*

1988

Sunday 15th May, 1988 at Old Trafford, Manchester
Widnes 38, St.Helens 14.
Widnes: Tries: *Wright (2), David Hulme (2), Tait, McKenzie, Sorensen.* **Goals:** *Currier (4), Platt.*
St.Helens: Tries: *Ledger, Haggerty,* **Goals:** *Loughlin (3).*
WIDNES: D.Platt; R.Thackray, A.Currier, D.Wright, M.Offiah; B.Dowd, David Hulme; K.Sorensen, P.McKenzie, J.Grima, M.O'Neill, Paul Hulme, R.Eyres.
Subs.: A.Tait (for Thackray), S.O'Neill (for Grima).
ST.HELENS: P.Loughlin; B.Ledger, D.Tanner, M.Elia, L.Quirk; M.Bailey, N.Holding; T.Burke, P.Groves, S.Evans, P.Forber, J.Fieldhouse, R.Haggerty.
Subs.: S.Allen (for Fieldhouse), B.Dwyer (for Evans).
Referee: Mr. J. Holdsworth (Kippax)
Attendance: 35,252. **Receipts:** *£232,298.*

1989

Sunday 14th May, 1989 at Old Trafford, Manchester
Widnes 18, Hull 10.
Widnes: Tries: *Wright, Currier, Offiah.*
Goals: *Davies (3)*
Hull: Try: *Welham.* **Goals:** *Pearce (3).*
WIDNES: A.Tait; J.Davies, A.Currier, D.Wright, M.Offiah; David Hulme, Paul Hulme; K.Sorensen, P.McKenzie, J.Grima, M.O'Neill, E.Koloto, R.Eyres.
Subs.: T.Myler (for D.Hulme), D.Pyke (for Currier).
HULL: P.Fletcher; P.Eastwood, B.Blacker, R.Price, D.O'Hara; G.Pearce, P.Windley; A.Dannatt, L.Jackson, S.Crooks, P.Welham, J.Sharp, G.Divorty.
Subs.: R.Nolan (for Windley), T.Wilby (for Price).
Referee: Mr, J. Holdsworth (Kippax)
Attendance: 40,194. **Receipts:** *£264,242.*

One of the great innovations which came as part of the League's new sponsorship deal with Stones Bitter was the introduction of a Premiership competition for the Second Division clubs, with the final staged as a curtain-raiser to the major Premiership Final. The

(*Above*) **Daryl Powell led Sheffield to glory in 1989.**

lure of playing at Old Trafford, and seeing the winners take their lap of honour in front of around 40,000 spectators, was a massive incentive for the Second Division clubs and it brought them enormous prestige.

And those clubs did not disappoint when given their opportunity to appear on the big stage, with all three Second Division Premiership Finals in the '80s producing games packed with thrills, open play and lots of tries. There was also some incredible drama with a nail-biting finish between Oldham and Featherstone in 1988, and a nice touch when the inaugral contestants in 1987 were Swinton and Hunslet, giants in the game's early history as two of only three clubs to win the coveted All Four Cups. In contrast, it was all about the new age of Rugby League when Sheffield Eagles, just five years old, captured their first major trophy in 1989.

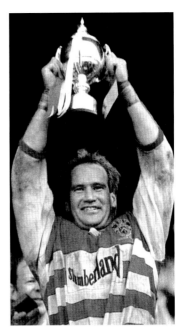

(*Above*) **Oldham captain Mal Graham, victorious at Old Trafford in 1988.**

SECOND DIVISION PREMIERSHIP FINALS IN THE ·80S

1987

Sunday 17th May, 1987 at Old Trafford, Manchester

Swinton 27, Hunslet 10.

Swinton: Tries: Bate, Derbyshire, Grima, Ainsworth, Lee. Goals: Rippon (3). Drop-goal: Les Holliday.
Hunslet: Tries: Bateman (2). Goal: Platt.
SWINTON: M.Viller; D.Bate, P.Topping, J.Brown, A.Rippon; S.Snape, M.Lee; J.Grima, G.Ainsworth, R.Muller, A.Derbyshire, Mike Holliday, Les Holliday.
Subs.: J.Allen (for M.Holliday), A.Ratcliffe (for Topping).
HUNSLET: A.Kay; P.Tate, C.Penola, J.Irvine, W.Wilson; G.Coates, G.King; A.Sykes, P.Gibson, A.Bateman, A.Platt, C.Bowden, G.Jennings.
Subs.: G.Senior (for Gibson), K.Mason (for Platt).
Referee: Mr. J. McDonald (Wigan).

1988

Sunday 15th May, 1988 at Old Trafford, Manchester

Oldham 28, Featherstone Rovers 26.

Oldham: Tries: Foy (2), Flanagan, Meadows, Walsh.
Goals: McAlister (4).
Featherstone: Tries: Steadman (2), Bannister, Sykes.
Goals: Quinn (5).
OLDHAM: M.Burke; P.Round, D.Foy, C.McAlister, K.Meadows; P.Walsh, M.Ford; I.Sharratt, I.Sanderson, H.Waddell, C.Hawkyard, M.Graham, T.Flanagan.
Subs.: R.Irving (for Burke), G.Warnecke (for Sherratt).
FEATHERSTONE: S.Quinn; A.Bannister, D.Sykes, A.Banks, R.Marsh; G.Steadman, D.Fox; G.Siddall, K.Bell, K.Harrison, P.Hughes, P.Smith, P.Lyman
Subs.: J.Crossley (for Marsh), J.Bastian (for Siddall).
Referee: Mr. R. Whitfield (Widnes).

(*Above*) **Swinton skipper Les Holliday and his team enjoy an Old Trafford lap of honour in 1987.**

1989

Sunday 14th May, 1989 at Old Trafford, Manchester

Sheffield Eagles 43, Swinton 18.

Sheffield: Tries: Powell (3), Broadbent, Aston, McDermott, Cook. Goals: Aston (7). Drop-goal: Aston.
Swinton: Tries: Frodsham, Melling, Ranson.
SHEFFIELD: M.Gamson; P.Cartwright, A.Dickinson, D.Powell, A.Young; M.Aston, D.Close; P.Broadbent, M.Cook, G.Van Bellen, S.Nickle, M.Fleming, W.Smith.
Subs.: S.Evans (for Close). P.McDermott (for Fleming).
SWINTON: P.Topping; S.Ranson, M.Viller, S.Snape, D.Bate; T.Frodsham, T.Hewitt; F.Mooney, A.Melling, S.O'Neill, G.Ainsworth, J,Allen, J.Myler.
Subs.: D.Maloney (for Viller), J.Horrocks (for Allen).
Referee: Mr. R. Whitfield (Widnes).

LANCASHIRE CUP FINALS

(Above, left) Barrow captain Alan Hodkinson is congratulated by his club chairman, Bob Brady, before being presented with the Lancashire Cup in 1983 by Mrs. Gilchrist, wife of the president of Burtonwood Brewery. (Above, right) Wigan skipper Graeme West and his team after their 1986 Final win over Oldham.

(Above) Skipper Ken Kelly and man-of-the-match Steve Hesford after Warrington's win in the 1982 Final.

Rugby League's boom during the second half of the 1980s was perfectly illustrated by the fortunes of the Lancashire Cup Final, which saw crowds rise dramatically on the back of Wigan's great revival. The first four Finals of the decade all were watched by crowds of less than 10,000 - maintaining the downward trend established during the 1970s - but when arch rivals Wigan and St.Helens met in the 1984 Lancashire Cup Final, both clubs armed with new signings from Australia, they knew the 16,000 capacity of the proposed venue at Wilderspool would not be enough to satisfy demand. They agreed to toss a coin, and Wigan won the opportunity to stage the Final at Central Park. The result was a 26,000 crowd - the biggest for a Lancashire Cup Final for 23 years - providing receipts of £62,139, more than four times the previous best. In an electric atmosphere, it was the Saints who prevailed, inspired by their Australian giant, Mal Meninga. Wigan came back from that disappointment to dominate the competition for the next four years

LANCASHIRE CUP FINALS IN THE '80s

1980

Sat. 4th October, 1980, at Knowsley Road, St.Helens

Warrington 26, Wigan 10.

Warrington: *Tries: Thackray, Bevan, Hesford, Martyn.* **Goals:** *Hesford (7).*

Wigan: *Tries: Fairbairn, Ramsdale.* **Goals:** *Fairbairn (2)*

WARRINGTON: D.Finnegan; R.Thackray, I.Duane, J.Bevan, S.Hesford; K.Kelly, A.Gwilliam; N.Courtney, A.Waller, B.Case, T.Martyn, R.Eccles, E.Hunter.

Subs.: I.Potter (for Eccles), A.Worrall (not used).

WIGAN: G.Fairbairn; D.Ramsdale, D.Willicombe, S.Davies, J.Hornby; M.Foy, L.Bolton; S.Breheny, J.Pendlebury, S.O'Neill, W.Melling, J.Clough, T.Hollingsworth.

Subs.: B.Coyle (for Bolton), M.Smith (for Pendlebury).

Referee: Mr. G. Kershaw (Easingwold)

Attendance: 6,279. Receipts: £8,966.

1981

Saturday 26th September, 1981, at Central Park, Wigan

Leigh 8, Widnes 3.

Leigh: *Try: Bilsbury.* **Goals:** *Woods (2).*

Drop-goal: *Donlan.*

Widnes: *Try: Bentley.*

LEIGH: M.Hogan; D.Drummond, T.Bilsbury, S.Donlan, G.Worgan; J.Woods, K.Green; A.Wilkinson, R.Tabern, T.Cooke, T.Martyn, G.Clarkson, M.McTigue.

Subs.: P.Fox (not used), W.Platt (for Martyn).

WIDNES: M.Burke; M.George, E.Hughes, E.Cunningham, K.Bentley; D.Moran, A.Gregory; M.O'Neill, K.Elwell, B.Lockwood, L.Gorley, E.Prescott, M.Adams.

Subs.: J.Myler, G.Shaw (neither used).

Referee: Mr. W. H. Thompson (Huddersfield)

Attendance: 9,011. Receipts: £14,029.

(Above) Wigan's Ian Potter faces up to Warrington's Bob Eccles in the 1985 Lancashire Cup Final, with Mike Ford and Steve Ella in support.

(Above) Harry Pinner leads the St.Helens celebrations after their win over Wigan in the 1984 Final, in front of 26,000 at Central Park.

with their huge following bringing big crowds to the Finals, all staged at Knowsley Road, St.Helens. The rise of the super powers in the game had been preceeded by one of the most romantic giant-killing acts, performed by Barrow in the 1983 Final. Then a second division side, Barrow beat the cup kings of Widnes with a memorable display. Sponsorship of the Lancashire Cup was rebranded in 1982 from Forshaws to Burtonwood.

1982

Saturday 23rd October, 1982, at Central Park, Wigan
Warrington 16, St.Helens 0.
Warrington: Tries: Fellows. Eccles, Mike Kelly, Ken Kelly.
Goals: Hesford (2).
WARRINGTON: S.Hesford; P.Fellows, R.Duane, J.Bevan, Mike Kelly; P.Cullen, Ken Kelly; N.Courtney, C.Webb, T.Cooke, R.Eccles, J.Fieldhouse, M.Gregory.
Subs.: D.Finnegan (not used), D.Chisnall (for Cooke).
ST.HELENS: B.Parkes; B.Ledger, C.Arkwright, R.Haggerty, D.Litherland; S.Peters, N.Holding; M.James, G.Liptrot, G.Bottell, G.Moorby, P.Gorley, H.Pinner.
Subs.: J.Smith (for Parkes), R.Mathias (for Bottell).
Referee: Mr. J. Holdsworth (Kippax)
Attendance: 6,462. Receipts: £11,732.

1983

Saturday 1st October, 1983, at Central Park, Wigan
Barrow 12, Widnes 8.
Barrow: Try: McConnell.
Goals: Ball (3). Drop-goals: Ball, Tickle.
Widnes: Try: Lydon. Goals: Lydon (2).
BARROW: S.Tickle; T.Moore, A.Whittle, I.Ball, D.Milby; R.McConnell, D.Cairns; A.Hodkinson, L.Wall, M.McJennett, S.Herbert, E.Szymala, S.Mossop.
Subs.: D.Elliott, D.Tyson (neither used).
WIDNES: M.Burke; J.Lydon, E.Hughes, K.O'Loughlin, J.Basnett; T.Myler, A.Gregory; S.O'Neill, K.Elwell, K.Tamati, F.Whitfield, E.Prescott, M.Adams.
Subs.: A.Garritty, P.Houghton (neither used).
Referee: Mr. K. Allatt (Southport)
Attendance: 7,007. Receipts: £13,160.

1984

Sunday 28th October, 1984, at Central Park, Wigan
St.Helens 26, Wigan 18.
St.Helens: Tries: Meninga (2), Haggerty, Day.
Goals: Day (5).
Wigan: Tries: Gill, West, Kiss. Goals: Whitfield (3).
ST.HELENS: P.Veivers; B.Ledger, S.Allen, M.Meninga, S.Day; C.Arkwright, N.Holding; T.Burke, G.Liptrot, P.Gorley, A.Platt, P.Round, H.Pinner.
Subs.: J.Smith (not used), R.Haggerty (for Veivers).
WIGAN: S.Edwards; J.Ferguson, D.Stephenson, C.Whitfield, H.Gill; M.Cannon, J.Fairhurst; N.Courtney, N.Kiss, B.Case, G.West, S.Wane, I.Potter.
Subs.: J.Pendlebury (for Gill), M.Scott (not used).
Referee: Mr. R. Campbell (Widnes)
Attendance: 26,074. Receipts: £62,139.

1985

Sunday 13th October, 1985 at Knowsley Road, St.Helens
Wigan 34, Warrington 8.
Wigan: Tries: Ella(2), Hanley, Kiss, Edwards.
Goals: Stephenson (7).
Warrington: Try: Johnson. Goals: Carbert (2).
WIGAN: S.Edwards; G.Henley-Smith, D.Stephenson, E.Hanley, C.Whitfield; S.Ella, M.Ford; G.Dowling, N.Kiss, S.Wane, N.Du Toit, A.Goodway, I.Potter.
Subs.: S.Hampson (for Henley-Smith), B.Case (for Wane).
WARRINGTON: B.Johnson; B.Carbert, P.Cullen, P.Blake, R.Thackray; K.Kelly, A.Gregory; R.Eccles, C.Webb, R.Jackson, L.Boyd, M.Gregory, A.Rathbone.
Subs.: M.Forster (for Blake), K.Tamati (for Boyd).
Referee: Mr. J. Holdsworth (Kippax)
Attendance: 19,202. Receipts: £56,030.

(Above) **Mike Ford scores in Wigan's 1986 win over his home town Oldham - Shaun Edwards and referee Jim Smith look on.**

Warrington managed to break Wigan's four year hold on the Lancashire Cup in 1989, but it was the brave beaten finalists, Oldham, who had seen off the men from Central Park with a 19-18 semi-final win. By this time the old competition went under the sponsorship banner of Grunhalle Lager, and the victorious Warrington side are pictured *(above)* led from the front by their captain, Mike Gregory.

1986

Sunday, 19th October, 1986 at Knowsley Road, St.Helens
Wigan 27, Oldham 6.
Wigan: Tries: *Edwards (2), Ford, Lydon.*
Goals: *Gill (5).* **Drop-goal:** *Lydon.*
Oldham: Try: *Bridge.* **Goal:** *Hobbs.*
WIGAN: S.Edwards; J.Lydon, D.Stepehenson, D.Bell, H.Gill; E.Hanley, M.Ford; G.West, M.Dermott, B.Case, I.Roberts, I.Potter, A.Goodway.
Subs.: S.Hampson (not used), R.Louw (for Roberts).
OLDHAM: H.M'Barki; P.Sherman, G.Bridge, G.Warnecke, M.Taylor; D.Topliss, P.Kirwan; B.Clark, T.Flanagan, D.Hobbs, T.Nadiole, M.Worrell, S.Raper.
Subs.: N.Clawson (not used), C.Hawkyard (for Raper).
Referee: *Mr. J. Smith (Halifax)*
Attendance: *20,180.* **Receipts:** *£60,329.*

1987

Sunday 11th October, 1987 at Knowsley Road, St.Helens
Wigan 28, Warrington 16.
Wigan: Tries: *Hanley (2), Gill, West.*
Goals: *Lydon (5), Stephenson.*
Warrington: Tries: *Forster (2), Gregory.*
Goals: *Woods (2)*
WIGAN: S.Hampson; R.Russell, D.Stephenson, J.Lydon, H.Gill; S.Edwards, A.Gregory; B.Case, N.Kiss S.Wane, A.Goodway, I.Potter, E.Hanley.
Subs.: D.Bell (for Stephenson), G.West (for Wane).
WARRINGTON: B.Johnson; D.Drummond, M.Forster, B.Peters, B.Carbert; J.Woods, K.Holden; K.Tamati, C.Webb, T.Humphries, G.Sanderson, M.Roberts, M.Gregory.
Subs.: D.Lyon (not used), N.Harmon (for Webb).
Referee: *Mr. F. Lindop (Wakefield)*
Attendance: *20,237.* **Receipts:** *£67,339.*

1988

Sunday 23rd October, 1988 at Knowsley Road, St.Helens
Wigan 22, Salford 17.
Wigan: Tries: *Kevin Iro (2), Shelford, Bell.*
Goals: *Kevin Iro (3).*
Salford: Tries: *Evans, Bentley, Herbert.*
Goals: *Brown (2).* **Drop-goal:** *Worrall.*
WIGAN: S.Hampson; Tony Iro, Kevin Iro, Bell, Lydon; S.Edwards, A.Gregory; I.Lucas, M.Dermott, A.Shelford, A.Platt, A.Goodway, E.Hanley.
Subs.: G.Byrne (for Lydon), D.Betts (for Lucas).
SALFORD: P.Williams; T.Evans, K.Bentley, K.Jones, A.Hadley; P.Shaw, D.Cairns; S.Herbert, M.Moran, P.Brown, I.Gormley, M.Worrall, M.Horo.
Subs.: I.Blease (for Williams), M.McTigue (for Horo).
Referee: *Mr. K. Allatt (Southport)*
Attendance: *19,154.* **Receipts:** *£71,879.*

1989

Saturday 14th October, 1989 at Knowsley Road, St.Helens
Warrington 24, Oldham 16.
Warrington: Tries: *Jackson (2), Ropati, Forster.*
Goals: *Turner (4).*
Oldham: Tries: *Robinson, Irving, Lord.* **Goals:** *Platt, Hyde.*
WARRINGTON: D.Lyon; D.Drummond, J.Ropati, T.Thorniley, M.Forster; R.Turner G.Mackey; T.Burke, M.Roskell, S.Molloy, R.Jackson, G.Sanderson, M.Gregory.
Subs.: P.Darbyshire (for Lyon), R.Duane (for Sanderson).
OLDHAM: D.Platt; S.Robinson, G.Hyde, R.Irving, P.Lord; B.Clark, M.Ford; L.Casey, A.Ruane, J.Fieldhouse, S.Allen, K.Newton, J.Cogger.
Subs.: R.Russell (for Platt), J.Fairbank (for Casey).
Referee: *Mr. R.Tennant (Castleford)*
Attendance: *9,990.* **Receipts:** *£41,804.*

THE MEN IN THE MIDDLE

(Above, left) Julien Rascagneres, the postman from Perpignan, shows Great Britain's Lee Crooks who's boss in the 1982 Ashes Third Test versus Australia at Headingley. *(Above, right)* Referee Ronnie Campbell gets his point across to Wigan coach Colin Clarke as Bradford Northern forward Geoff Clarkson looks on.

New horizons opened up for the game's top referees when the decision was taken to have officials from 'neutral' countries control Test matches, starting in 1981. This came in the aftermath of the two controversial clashes between England and France in 1980 and '81, in which visiting referees Billy Thompson and Guy Cattaneo left the host nations fuming. Not that the first Australian referee sent over to take charge of the two Great Britain-France Tests in December 1981 was any stranger to controversy - Greg Hartley was not nicknamed 'Hollywood' for nothing.

Frenchman Julien Rascagneres, a postman from Perpignan - a hooker in his playing days - became the first 'neutral' to referee an Ashes series in 1982 as Great Britain were humbled by the 'Invincible' Kangaroos. Rascagneres was a popular figure with his firm control and clear decisions easily surmounting the language barrier, and the Australians liked him so much they invited him to take charge of their 1985 three-match series against New Zealand rather than have an English referee. Rascagneres refereed his second Ashes series in 1986, and this was followed by another French official, Francis Desplas, taking the 1988 Ashes in Australia. Fred Lindop became the first English referee to control a full series down-under in 1982 when he took the two Tests in Australia with the Kiwis. Lindop's long and much decorated career came to an end in 1988 when he refereed the Challenge Cup Final 18 years after his first Wembley appearance in 1970, and some 21 years since he had the whistle in the 1967 Ashes. Fred reached the RFL's mandatory retirement age in 1988 and, after hanging up his whistle, was appointed their first Referees' Controller. Robin Whitfield followed him in refereeing Tests both in Australia and in France, and by the end of the decade John Holdsworth had established himself as the game's top referee. Widnes based Ronnie Campbell had the distinction of refereeing the epic 1985 Wigan-Hull Wembley Cup Final.

Get Off!
and see the competitive terms available for most types of motor, fire, accident and marine insurance from
Dominion Insurance
SPONSORS OF GREAT BRITAIN RUGBY LEAGUE
Northern Region

(Above) Fred Lindop helping to advertise the international game's sponsors in 1983.

WEMBLEY REFEREES

1980 - **Fred Lindop** (Wakefield)
1981 - **Gerry Kershaw** (Easingwold)
1982 - **Fred Lindop** (Wakefield) *
1983 - **Robin Whitfield** (Widnes)
1984 - **Billy Thompson** (Huddersfield)
1985 - **Ron Campbell** (Widnes)
1986 - **Robin Whitfield** (Widnes)
1987 - **John Holdsworth** (Kippax)
1988 - **Fred Lindop** (Wakefield)
1989 - **Ray Tennant** (Castleford)
* *Lindop also refereed the 1982 replay.*

YORKSHIRE CUP FINALS

(Right)
The perfect scenario for a Yorkshire Cup Final - Headingley on a lovely autumn Saturday afternoon in October. This was in 1986 and Castleford had just beaten Hull to win the old county trophy, as their captain John Joyner and scrum-half Bob Beardmore, winner of the White Rose trophy as man-of-the-match, pose for the photographers on the cricket ground side of the grandstand.
John Joyner was very familiar with Yorkshire Cup Finals throughout the decade of the 1980s, appearing in no less than seven, which included a replay. He lifted the trophy as the winning captain just twice.

The Yorkshire Cup broke new ground during the 1980s - several new grounds, in fact, as the former sponsor's insistence that the Final be staged at Headingley, even if Leeds were in it - a bugbear for the Yorkshire County committee for much of the previous decade- was overcome. For the more 'low key' events, there was still nothing more enjoyable,

YORKSHIRE CUP FINALS IN THE '80s

1980
Saturday 8th November, 1980 at Fartown, Huddersfield
Leeds 8, Hull Kingston Rovers 7.
Leeds: Try: A.Smith. Goals: Dick (2). Drop-goal: Dick.
Hull K.R.: Try: McHugh. Goals: Hogan (2).
LEEDS: W.Oulton; A.Smith, D.Smith, N.Hague, J.Atkinson; J.Holmes, K.Dick; M.Harrison, D.Ward, S.Pitchford, G.Eccles, P.Cookson, D.Heron.
Subs.: J.Carroll (for Cookson)
HULL K.R.: I.Robinson; G.McHugh, M.Smith, P.Hogan, W.Youngman; D.Hall, P.Harkin; R.Holdstock, R.Price, S.Crooks, P.Lowe, L.Casey, M.Crane. *Subs.:* P.Rose (for Crooks)
Referee: Mr. R.Campbell (Widnes)
Attendance: 9,751. Receipts: £15,578.

1981
Saturday 3rd October, 1981 at Headingley, Leeds
Castleford 10, Bradford Northern 5.
Castleford: Tries: Hyde, Joyner. Goals: Finch (2).
Bradford Northern: Try: Parker. Goal: Hanley.
CASTLEFORD: G.Claughton; T.Richardson, S.Fenton, G.Hyde, G.Morris; J.Joyner, R.Beardmore; A.Hardy, R.Spurr, B.Johnson, D.Finch, K.Ward, A.Timson.
Subs.: P.Norton (for Hardy)
BRADFORD: K.Mumby; D.Barends, G.Hale, A.Parker, L.Gant; E.Hanley, A.Redfearn; J.Grayshon, B.Noble, P.Sanderson, G.Van Bellen, G.Idle, A.Rathbone.
Subs.: D.Redfearn (for Sanderson), D.Jasiewicz (for Van Bellen).
Referee: Mr. R. Whitfield (Widnes)
Attendance: 5,852. Receipts: £10,359.

or traditional, than a Yorkshire Cup Final at Headingley on a balmy autumn Saturday afternoon, but the rise of the Humberside super powers in the early '80s meant pastures new had to be sought on some occasions to satisfy public demand. And so some Yorkshire Cup Finals found themselves being staged on major football grounds after that ice had been re-broken by the replay of the 1982 Challenge Cup Final at Elland Road. But not before the decade had begun with the once mighty surroundings of Fartown seeing Yorkshire's finest do battle for the county cup, Leeds beating favourites Hull K.R. by one point following an inspired display by Kevin Dick.

Hull returned to Elland Road, scene of their Challenge Cup night of glory, to win the 1983 Yorkshire Cup Final against Castleford in what proved to be the middle one of a hat-trick of Yorkshire Cups for the 'Airlie Birds', the highlight of which was the 1984 Final against local rivals Hull K.R. at Boothferry Park. home of the city's football club Hull City. That match drew a crowd of 25,237, the biggest attendance for a Yorkshire Cup Final since way back in 1958, and they saw Hull stage a remarkable second-half comeback - led by their all-international back division guided by great Australian scrum-half Peter Sterling, to defeat the Robins and bring joy to the west of the city.

(Above) **John Atkinson of Leeds in action in the 1980 Yorkshire Cup Final which they won against Hull K.R. at Fartown, Huddersfield.**

1982

Saturday 2nd October, 1982 at Headingley, Leeds
Hull 18, Bradford Northern 7.
Hull: Tries: Rose (2), Evans, Prendiville.
Goals: Crooks (2). Drop-goals: Crooks (2).
Bradford Northern: Try: Whiteman.
Goal: Carroll. Drop-goal: Carroll.
HULL: G.Kemble; S.Evans, T.Day, J.Leuluai, P.Prendiville; D.Topliss, K.Harkin; T.Skerrett, J.Bridges, R.Stone, P.Rose, L.Crooks, M.Crane.
Subs.: S.Norton (for Crane)
BRADFORD: K.Mumby; D.Barends, L.Gant, A.Parker, S.Pullen; K.Whiteman, D.Carroll; J.Grayshon, B.Noble, G. Van Bellen, G.Idle, D.Jasiewicz, G.Hale.
Subs.: D.Smith (for Pullen), P.Sanderson (for Van Bellen).
Referee: Mr. S. Wall (Leigh)
Attendance: 11,755. Receipts: £21,950.

1983

Saturday 15th October, 1983 at Elland Road, Leeds
Hull 13, Castleford 2.
Hull: Tries: O'Hara, Crane, Proctor. Drop-goal: Crane.
Castleford: Goal: Beardmore.
HULL: G.Kemble; P.Solal, G.Schofield, J.Leuluai, D.O'Hara; D.Topliss, T.Dean; P.Edmonds, R.Wileman, T.Skerrett, W.Proctor, L.Crooks, M.Crane.
Subs.: B.Banks, P.Rose (neither used).
CASTLEFORD: D.Coen; S.Fenton, T.Marchant, G.Hyde, J.Kear; J.Joyner, R.Beardmore; G.Connell, S.Horton, M.Reilly, A.Timson, N.James, K.England.
Subs.: I.Orum (for Hyde), A.Hardy (not used).
Referee: Mr. W. H. Thompson (Huddersfield)
Attendance: 14,049. Receipts: £33,572.

1984

Saturday 27th October, 1984 at Boothferry Park, Hull
Hull 29, Hull Kingston Rovers 12.
Hull: Tries: Kemble (2), Norton, Crooks, Evans.
Goals: Schofield (4). Drop-goal: Schofield.
Hull Kingston Rovers: Tries: Robinson, Fairbairn, Hall.
HULL: G.Kemble; J.Leuluai, G.Schofield, S.Evans, D.O'Hara; F.Ah Kuoi, P.Sterling; P.Edmonds, S.Patrick, L.Crooks, S.Norton, W.Proctor, G.Divorty.
Subs.: D.Topliss (not used), P.Rose (for Divorty).
HULL K.R.: G.Fairbairn; G.Clark, I.Robinson, G.Prohm, D.Laws; M.Smith, P.Harkin; M.Broadhurst, D.Watkinson, A.Ema, C.Burton, A.Kelly, D.Hall.
Subs.: S.Hartley (for Ema), C.Rudd (for Harkin).
Referee: Mr. F. Lindop (Wakefield)
Attendance: 25,237. Receipts: £68,639.

1985

Sunday 27th October, 1985 at Headingley, Leeds
Hull Kingston Rovers 22, Castleford 18.
Hull Kingston Rovers: Tries: Miller (2), Clark.
Goals: Dorahy (5).
Castleford: Tries: Marchant (2), R.Beardmore.
Goals: R.Beardmore (2). Diamond.
HULL K.R.: G.Fairbairn; G.Clark, J.Dorahy, G.Prohm, D.Laws; G.Smith, P.Harkin; D.Harrison, D.Watkinson, A.Ema, C.Burton, P.Hogan, G.Miller.
Subs.: J.Lydiat (for Fairbairn), A.Kelly (for Hogan).
CASTLEFORD: G.Lord; D.Plange, T.Marchant, G.Hyde, C.Spears; S.Diamond, R.Beardmore; K.Ward, K.Beardmore, B.Johnson, K.England, M.Ketteridge, J.Joyner. *Subs.:* D.Roockley, S.Horton (neither used).
Referee: Mr. R. Campbell (Widnes).
Attendance: 12,686. Receipts: 36,327.

The Yorkshire Cup had been the first of the game's old competitions to take on a sponsor's name in the 1970s, and this continued throughout the '80s - first with the Yorkshire brewers Websters, then in 1983 and '84 Phillips Video, and then a long running association with another Yorkshire brewery, John Smiths, commencing in 1985. The highlight of their time as sponsors came in 1988 with a magnificent occasion at the Leeds United stadium, Elland Road, when almost 23,000 people turned out to see Leeds beat Castleford in a Final full of sparkling rugby, after which Lee Crooks lifted the trophy for the Loiners.

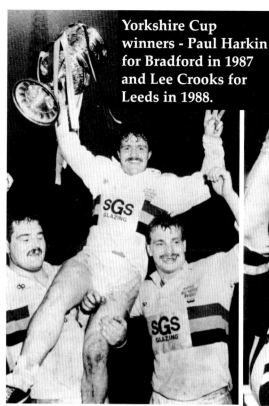

Yorkshire Cup winners - Paul Harkin for Bradford in 1987 and Lee Crooks for Leeds in 1988.

1986

Saturday 11th October, 1986 at Headingley, Leeds

Castleford 31, Hull 24.

Castleford: Tries: K.Beardmore (2), Ketteridge, Atkins, Ward. *Goals:* Ketteridge (5). *Drop-goal:* R.Beardmore.
Hull: Tries: O'Hara (2), Brand (2). *Goals:* Crooks (4).
CASTLEFORD: C.Scott; D.Plange, T.Marchant, C.Johns, G.Hyde; J.Joyner, R.Beardmore; K.Ward, K.Beardmore, B.Johnson, M.Ketteridge, B.Atkins.
Subs.: G.Lord (for Hyde), A.Shillito (for Atkins).
HULL: G.Kemble; M.Brand, G.Schofield, D.O'Hara, P.Eastwood; F.Ah Kuoi, P.Windley; D.Brown, S.Patrick, A.Dannatt, S.Norton, L.Crooks, J.Sharp.
Subs.: G.Divorty (for Norton), N.Puckering (for Brown).
Referee: Mr. J. McDonald (Wigan)
Attendance: 11,132. Receipts: £31,888.

(Left) Castleford captain John Joyner with the Yorkshire Cup in 1981. He would go on to lead Castleford to victory in the white rose final again in 1986.

1987

Saturday 17th October, 1987 at Headingley, Leeds

Bradford Northern 12, Castleford 12.

Bradford:Try: Fairbank. *Goals:* Mumby (2), Hobbs (2).
Castleford: Tries: Plange, Lindner. *Goals:* Ketteridge (2).
BRADFORD: G.Mercer; P.Ford, S.McGowan, R.Simpson, R.Francis; K.Mumby, P.Harkin; J.Grayshon, B.Noble, B.Hill, K.Skerrett, K.Fairbank, T.Holmes.
Subs.: N.Roebuck (for Holmes), D.Hobbs (for Grayshon).
CASTLEFORD: D.Roockley; D.Plange, T.Marchant, M.Beattie, G.Hyde; J.Joyner, R.Southerwood; A.Shillito, K.Beardmore, K.Ward, M.Ketteridge, J.Fifita, R.Lindner. *Subs.:* R.Beardmore (for Shillito), D.Sampson (for K.Beardmore).
Referee: Mr. K. Allatt (Southrport).
Attendance: 10,947. Receipts: £40,283.

1987 - Replay

Saturday 31st October, 1987 at Elland Road, Leeds

Bradford Northern 11, Castleford 2.

Bradford: Tries: Hill, Heron.
Goal: Hobbs. *Drop-goal:* Hobbs.
Castleford: Goal: Ketteridge.
BRADFORD: K.Mumby; P.Ford, S.McGowan, G.Mercer, R.Simpson; R.Stewart, P.Harkin; D.Hobbs, B.Noble, B.Hill, K.Skerrett, K.Fairbank, W.Heron.
Subs.: N.Roebuck, D.Redfearn (neither used).
CASTLEFORD: D.Roockley; D.Plange, T.Marchant, M.Beattie, G.Hyde; R.Southernwood, R.Beardmore; K.Ward, K.Hill, J.Fifita, M.Ketteridge, K.England, J.Joyner. *Subs.:* G.Boothroyd (for England), D.Sampson (for Fifita).
Referee: Mr. K. Allatt (Southport)
Attendance: 8,175. Receipts: £30,732.

(*Above*) **Garry Schofield skips past Castleford scrum-half Bob Beardmore in the 1983 Yorkshire Cup Final at Elland Road, which the 'Airlie Birds' won 13-2. In support of Schofield is winger Patrick Solal, who became the first French player to take part in a Yorkshire Cup Final. It was Schofield's first major honour in a sensational debut season in the professional ranks and Hull went on to retain the famous old trophy the following year in 1984 to make it a hat-trick of wins.** (*Right*) **Bradford Northern's 'super sub' Paul Medley tries to beat Featherstone's Paul Newlove in the 1989 Final at Headingley. Bradford, with scrum-half Paul Harkin their star, won the trophy twice in three years.**

1988

Sunday 16th October, 1988 at Elland Road, Leeds
Leeds 33, Castleford 12.
Leeds: Tries: Schofield (2), Gibson (2), Medley.
*Goals: Stephenson (6). **Drop-goal:** Schofield.*
Castleford: Tries: Boothroyd, Joyner. **Goals:** *Ketteridge (2).*
LEEDS: G.Spencer; A.Ettingshausen, G.Schofield, D.Stephenson, C.Gibson; C.Lyons, R.Ashton; L.Crooks, C.Maskill, H.Waddell, R.Powell, M.Brooke-Cowden, D.Heron. *Subs.:* P.Medley (for Brooke-Cowden), S.Backo (for Waddell).
CASTLEFORD: G.Belcher; D.Plange, T.Marchant, G.Boothroyd, C.Chapman; G.Anderson, R.Beardmore; K.Ward, K.Beardmore, K.England, M.Ketteridge, R.Gibbs, J.Joyner. *Subs.:* D.Roockley (for Chapman), D.Sampson (for Roockley).
Referee: Mr. R. Whitfield (Widnes).
Attendance: 22,968. Receipts: £76,658.

1989

Sunday 5th Ovember, 1989 at Headingley, Leeds
Bradford Northern 20, Featherstone R. 14.
Bradford: Tries: Cordle (2), Harkin (2).
Goals: Hobbs (2).
Featherstone: Tries: Ropati, Smith.
Goals: Fox (3).
BRADFORD: I.Wilkinson; G.Cordle, S.McGowan, R.Simpson, R.Francis; I.Henjak, P.Harkin; K.Skerrett, G.Barraclough, J.Hamer, D.Hobbs, K.Fairbank, J.Pendlebury. *Subs.:* K.Mumby (for Henjak), P.Medley (for Hamer).
FEATHERSTONE: C.Bibb; Drummond, I.Ropati, P.Newlove, A.Banks; I.Smales, D.Fox; J.Grayshon, T.Clark, G.Bell, G.Price, C.Booth, P.Smith.
Subs.: A.Dakin (for Bell), A.Fisher (for Booth).
Referee: Mr. R. Whitfield (Widnes).
Attendance: 12,607. Receipts: £50,775.

JOHN PLAYER TROPHY FINALS

(*Above*) **Ken Kelly and Steve Hesford enjoy showing the John Player Trophy after Warrington's win over Barrow in the 1981 Final.**
(*Above, right*) **Wigan captain Colin Whitfield and his team celebrate after victory over Leeds in the 1983 Final.**

The John Player Trophy, which had been launched in 1971-72, really came of age during the '80s as a mid-season knockout tournament which brought nationwide television coverage for the sport and sponsorship funds for the clubs. It also provided moments on the big stage for some for whom dreams of a Wembley final were unlikely to be fulfilled again, not least Barrow - who qualified for the 1981 John Player Trophy Final after a memorable semi-final win over Hull and went on to give Warrington a tough challenge. Attendances were much bigger for the finals than in the previous decade, especially when the two Humberside clubs came face to face - as they did twice, both times drawing crowds of over 25,000. The first of those all-Hull showdowns was at Headingley in 1982, with a re-match in their own city at Boothferry Park in 1985 on a famously snow-covered pitch.

JOHN PLAYER TROPHY FINALS IN THE '80s

1980

Saturday 5th January, 1980, at Headingley, Leeds
Bradford Northern 6, Widnes 0.
Bradford Northern: Try: Parker.
Goal: Mumby. Drop-goal: Stephenson.
BRADFORD NORTHERN: K.Mumby; D.Barends, D.Redfearn, D.Parker, L.Gant; N.Stephenson, A.Redfearn; J.Thompson, J.Bridges, C.Forsyth, J.Grayshon, G.Van Bellen, L.Casey. *Subs.:* S.Ferres (for G.Van Bellen), I.Van Bellen (for Forsyth).
WIDNES: D.Eckersley; S.Wright, M.Aspey, M.George, M.Burke; E.Hughes, R.Bowden; B.Hogan, K.Elwell, G.Shaw, L.Gorley, D.Hull, M.Adams. *Subs.:* J.Mills (for Hogan), Alan Dearden (not used).
Referee: Mr. W. H. Thompson (Huddersfield)
Attendance: 9,909. Receipts: £11,560.

1981

Saturday 24th January, 1981, at Central Park, Wigan
Warrington 12, Barrow 5.
Warrington: Tries: Bevan (2).
Goals: Hesford (2). Drop-goals: Hesford (2).
Barrow: Try: Mason. Goal: Ball.
WARRINGTON: S.Hesford; R.Thackray, I.Duane, J.Bevan, M.Kelly; K.Kelly, A.Gwilliam; N.Courtney, A.Waller, B.Case, T.Martyn, I.Potter, E.Hunter. *Subs.:* J.Fairhurst (not used), R.Eccles (for Hunter).
BARROW: D.Elliott; R.McConnell, N.French, I.Ball, A.Wainwright; M.Mason, D.Cairns; D.Chisnall, H.Allen, M.Flynn, K.James, S.Kirkby, D.Hadley. *Subs.:* M.James (not used), E.Syzmala (for Allen).
Referee: Mr. W. H. Thompson (Huddersfield)
Attendance: 12,820. Receipts: £21,020.

(*Left*) Gavin Miller, on the attack as Hull K.R. beat city rivals Hull in the snow in the 1985 Final at Boothferry Park. Rovers' Mark Broadhurst looks on as Gary Divorty makes the tackle.

1982

Saturday 23rd January, 1982, at Headingley, Leeds

Hull 12, Hull Kingston Rovers 4.

Hull: Try: Wileman.
Goals: Crooks (4). *Drop-goals:* Dean (2).
Hull K.R.: Goals: Fairbairn (2).
HULL: B.Banks; D.O'Hara, C.Harrison, J.Leuluai, P.Prendiville; T.Day, T.Dean; T.Skerrett, R.Wileman, R.Stone, M.Crane, L.Crooks, S.Norton.
Subs.: K.Harkin (for Dean), S.Lloyd (not used).
HULL K.R.: G.Fairbairn; S.Hubbard, M.Smith, P.Hogan, P.Muscroft; S.Hartley, P.Harkin; R.Holdstock, D.Watkinson, S.Crooks, P.Lowe, L.Casey, D.Hall.
*Subs.:*C.Burton (for Harkin), J.Millington (for Holdstock).
Referee: Mr. F. Lindop (Wakefield)
Attendance: 25,165. *Receipts: £42,987.*

1983

Saturday 22nd January, 1983, at Elland Road, Leeds

Wigan 15, Leeds 4.

Wigan: Tries:: Gill, Juliff.
Goals: Whitfield (4). *Drop-goal:* Whitfield.
Leeds: Goals: Dick (2).
WIGAN: B.Williams, D.Ramsdale, D.Stephenson, C.Whitfield, H.Gill; M.Foy, J.Fairhurst; G.Shaw, N.Kiss, D.Campbell, G.West, M.Scott, J.Pendlebury.
Subs.: B.Juliff (for Gill), B.Case (for West).
LEEDS: N.Hague; M.Campbell, I.Wilkinson, L.Dyl, Andy Smith; J.Holmes, K.Dick; R.Dickinson, D.Ward, T.Burke, A.Sykes, W.Heron, D.Heron.
Subs.: M.Conway, D.Heselwood (neither used).
Referee: Mr. R. Campbell (Widnes)
Attendance: 19,553. *Receipts: £49,027.*

1984

Saturday 14th January, 1984, at Central Park, Wigan

Leeds 18, Widnes 10.

Leeds: Tries: Holmes, Dick.
Goals: Creasser (5).
Widnes: Tries: Linton, Lydon. *Goal:* Burke.
LEEDS: I.Wilkinson; P.Prendiville, D.Creasser, D.Bell, Andy Smith; J.Holmes, K.Dick; Keith Rayne, D.Ward, Kevin Rayne, G.Moorby, M.Laurie, T.Webb.
Subs.: N.Hague(not used), K.Squire (for Ward)
WIDNES: M.Burke; S.Wright, Keiron O'Loughlin, J,Lydon, R.Linton; E.Hughes, A.Gregory; S.O'Neill, K.Elwell, K.Tamati, L.Gorley, F.Whitfield, M.Adams.
Subs.: J.Myler, E.Prescott (neither used).
Referee: Mr. W. H. Thompson (Huddersfield)
Attendance: 9,510. *Receipts: £19,824.*

1985

Saturday 26th January, 1985, at Boothferry Park, Hull

Hull Kingston Rovers 12, Hull 0.

Hull K.R.: Tries: Prohm, Hogan, Clark.
HULL K.R.: G.Fairbairn; G.Clark, I.Robinson, G.Prohm, D.Laws; M.Smith, P.Harkin; M.Broadhurst, D.Watkinson, A.Ema, C.Burton, P.Hogan, G.Miller.
Subs.: J.Lydiat, L.Casey (neither used).
HULL: G.Kemble; S.Evans, F.Ah Kuoi, J.Leuluai, D.O'Hara; D.Topliss, P.Sterling; P.Edmonds, S.Patrick, P.Rose, L.Crooks, W.Proctor, G.Divorty.
Subs.: G.Schofield (for Kemble), A.Dannatt (for Edmonds).
Referee: Mr. S. Wall (Leigh)
Attendance: 25,326. *Receipts: £69,555.*

Wigan proved to be the decade's most prolific winners of the John Player Trophy, lifting it four times - the first of those victorious finals coming in 1983 and acting as a kick-start for Wigan as a major trophy winning club after a barren era for the cherry and whites. Their coach at that time was Alex Murphy, and by the latter part of the '80s, the Kiwi Graham Lowe had taken the reins at Central Park and was presiding over the glory days. Lowe's first triumph in the competition came in 1987 at Burnden Park, the home of Bolton Wanderers, and the venue was the same two years later as the feat was repeated against pre-match favourites Widnes. Another of the game's charismatic coaching figures, Maurice Bamford, finally got his hands on some major silverware when his Leeds team won the trophy in 1984, after a final at Wigan marred by severe gale-force winds which were so strong they blew down one of the goal-posts. Leeds fared less well four years later at the same venue on a heavy pitch, as Neil Holding's drop-goal won it for St.Helens.

(Above) **The Leeds coach Maurice Bamford holds the John Player Trophy in his victorious team's dressing room after their win over Widnes at Wigan in the 1984 final.**

1986

Saturday 11th January, 1986 at Elland Road, Leeds
Wigan 11, Hull Kingston Rovers 8.
Wigan: Tries: *Wane, Ford.*
Goals: *Stephenson.* **Drop-goal:** *Dowling.*
Hull K.R.: Tries: *Lydiat, Laws.*
WIGAN: S.Hampson; R.Mordt, D.Stephenson, E.Hanley, H.Gill; S.Ella, M.Ford; G.Dowling, N.Kiss, S.Wane, G.West, A.Goodway, I.Potter.
Subs.: S.Edwards (for Gill), N.Du Toit (for Potter).
HULL K.R.: J.Lydiat; G.Clark, M.Smith, J.Dorahy, D.Laws; G.Smith, P.Harkin; P.Johnston, D.Watkinson, A.Ema, C.Burton, A.Kelly, G.Miller.
Subs.: I.Robinson (for Johnston), C.Rudd (not used).
Referee: *Mr. J. Holdsworth (Kippax)*
Attendance: *17,573.* **Receipts:** *£66,714.*

1987

Saturday 10th January, 1987 at Burnden Park, Bolton
Wigan 18, Warrington 4.
Wigan: Tries: *Gill (2), Goodway, Bell.* **Goal:** *Gill.*
Warrington: Try: *Forster.*
WIGAN: S.Hampson; D.Stephenson, J.Lydon, D.Bell, H.Gill; E.Hanley, S.Edwards; G.West, M.Dermott, B.Case, I.Roberts, I.Potter, A.Goodway.
Subs.: M.Ford, R.Louw (neither used).
WARRINGTON: B.Johnson; K.Meadows, P.Cullen, J.Ropati, M.Forster; K.Kelly, S.Peters; L.Boyd, K.Tamati, R.Jackson, G.Sanderson, M.Roberts, M.Gregory.
Subs.: R.Duane (for Peters), A.Rathbone (for Tamati).
Referee: *Mr. J. Holdsworth (Kippax)*
Attendance: *21,144.* **Receipts:** *£ 86,041.*

1988

Saturday 9th January, 1988, at Central Park, Wigan
St.Helens 15, Leeds 14.
St.Helens: Tries: *Loughlin (2).*
Goals: *Loughlin (3).* **Drop-goal:** *Holding.*
Leeds: Tries: *Creasser, Jackson.* **Goals:** *Creasser (3).*
ST.HELENS: P.Veivers; D.Tanner, P.Loughlin, M.Elia, L.Quirk; S.Cooper, N.Holding; T.Burke, P.Groves, P.Souto, P.Forber, R.Haggerty, A.Platt.
Subs.: D.Large (not used), S.Evans (for Souto).
LEEDS: M.Gurr; S.Morris, G.Schofield, P.Jackson, J.Basnett; D.Creasser, R.Ashton; P.Tunks, C.Maskill, Kevin Rayne, R.Powell, P.Medley, D.Heron.
Subs.: C.Gibson (for Basnett), J.Fairbank (for Rayne).
Referee: *Mr. F. Lindop (Wakefield)*
Attendance: *16,669.* **Receipts:** *£62,232.*

1989

Saturday 7th January, 1989 at Burnden Park, Bolton
Wigan 12, Widnes 6.
Wigan: Tries: *Kevin Iro, Hanley.* **Goals:** *Lydon (2).*
Widnes: Try: *Wright.* **Goal:** *Currier.*
WIGAN: S.Hampson; D.Bell, Kevin Iro, Lydon, Tony Iro; G.Byrne, S.Edwards; A.Shelford, M.Dermott, S.Wane, D.Betts, I.Potter, E.Hanley.
Subs.: A.Grgeory (for Lydon), A.Goodway (for Shelford).
WIDNES: A.Tait; R.Thackray, A.Currier, D.Wright, M.Offiah; T.Myler, David Hulme; K.Sorensen, P.McKenzie, J.Grima, M.O'Neill, E.Koloto, R.Eyres.
Subs.: B.Dowd (not used), Paul Hulme (for Koloto).
Referee: *Mr. J. Holdsworth (Kippax)*
Attendance: *20,709.* **Receipts:** *£94,874.*

THE CHARITY SHIELD

The Isle of Man was new ground for Rugby League when the Charity Shield was introduced in 1985, sponsored by Okells brewery and played at the Douglas Bowl. It was a pleasant trip for supporters and an enjoyable pre-season game between the Challenge Cup and Championship winners. After four years on the Isle of Man, the RFL realised the potential to develop the fixture into something much bigger and in August 1989 the Charity Shield came back to the mainland, with a 17,263 crowd at Liverpool Football Club's Anfield stadium and live television coverage by Granada T.V., plus a new sponsorship deal with C.I.S. (insurance). They saw a thriller as Champions Widnes defeated Cup holders Wigan. Pictured *(right)* is the Widnes captain Kurt Sorensen receiving the last Okells Charity Shield on the Isle of Man in 1988.

1985 - **Wigan 34, Hull K.R. 6.** *(Isle of Man)* - 4,066
1986 - **Halifax 9, Castleford 8.** *(Isle of Man)* - 3,276
1987 - **Wigan 44, Halifax 12.** *(Isle of Man)* - 4,804
1988 - **Widnes 20, Wigan 14.** *(Isle of Man)* - 5,044
1989 - **Widnes 27, Wigan 22.** *(Liverpool)* - 17,263

OTHER INTERNATIONAL ADVENTURES

In addition to the regular tours by Kangaroos and Kiwis, along with annual Test matches with France, Rugby League enjoyed several other international adventures during the 1980s. The city of Venice was the scene of a fiesty encounter between the full Great Britain and France teams in July 1982, as attempts were made to revive interest in the game in Italy. The French won 8-7.

(Above) **Programme for the match in Venice in 1982 between Britain and France.**

Other touring teams which came to England to play professional teams are listed *(below)*, meanwhile BARLA hosted the New Zealand Maori in 1983, the Junior Kiwis in 1987 and a couple of Australian Highschools tours. Two English clubs ventured down-under, Hull as Champions in 1983 and St.Helens as Premiership winners in 1985, although both went with weakened teams. Also, both the Penrith club and Queensland Residents toured to France.

Hull F.C. tour 1983
In New Zealand
Auckland 28, Hull 28.
N.Z. Maori 16, Hull 4.
In Australia
Newcastle 22, Hull 8.
Souths (Dapto) 22, Hull 24.

St.Helens tour 1985
In New Zealand
Canterbury 30, St.Helens 24.
Waikato 34, St.Helens 24.
Manukau 26, St.Helens 10.
Northern Dist. 12, St.Helens 42.

France tour 1982
Sept.22 - **Oldham 11, France 15.** *Att. 1,160*
Sept.24 - **Featherstone 5, France 13.** *Att. 840*
Sept.26 - **Wigan 11, France 7.** *Att. 3,700*

Queensland State tour 1983
Oct. 16 - **Hull K.R. 8, Queensland 6.** *Att. 6,383*
Oct. 23 - **Wigan 2, Queensland 40.** *Att.9,749*
Oct. 29 - **Leeds 2, Queensland 58.** *Att. 5,647*

Auckland tour 1987
Oct. 25 - **Leeds 25, Auckland 29.** *Att. 6,639*
Oct. 27 - **Warrington 16, Auckland 22.** *Att. 3,897*
Nov. 1 - **St.Helens 52, Auckland 26.** *Att. 5,901*
Nov. 4 - **Hull 26, Auckland 24.** *Att. 1,921*
Nov. 8 - **Wigan 6, Auckland 10.** *Att. 10,743*
Nov.10 - **Chairman's X111 12, Auckland 6.** *Att.3,636*

Papua New Guinea Kumuls tour 1987
Oct. 11 - **Featherstone 16, Kumuls 22.** *Att. 3,315*
Oct. 14 - **Lancashire 22, Kumuls 22.** *Att. 4,202*
Oct. 18 - **Swinton 13, Kumuls 6.** *Att. 2,132*
Oct. 20 - **Cumbria 22, Kumuls 4.** *Att. 3,750*
Oct. 24 - **GREAT BRITAIN 42, P.N.G. 0.** *Att. 9,121*
Oct. 27 - **Yorkshire 28, Kumuls 4.** *Att. 1,908*
Oct. 30 - **BARLA X111 16, Kumuls 20.** *Att. 2,700*
Nov. 1 - **Fulham 4, Kumuls 12.** *Att. 1,216*
(The Papua Guinea team went on to France where they played 4, won 1, lost 2 and drew 1, including losing the solitary Test match versus France 21-4.)

France tour 1988
Oct. 16 - **Warrington 6, France 29.** *Att. 3,200*
Oct. 19 - **Cumbria 18, France 13.** *Att. 4,000*
Oct. 23 - **Halifax 24, France 18.** *Att. 4,674*

THE GAME IN AUSTRALIA

(Right)
The style of Rugby League in Australia in the late 1980s, as 'E.T.' (pin-up boy Andrew Ettingshausen) plays for Cronulla versus Balmain, wearing the kits which became a craze for fans in Britain and playing a game which became a craze for coaches across the world.

(Above)
Arthur Beetson leads Queensland out for the very first State of Origin match as a legend was born at Lang Park in 1980.

The turnaround in the fortunes of Rugby League in Australia during the 1980s was quite dramatic as it set a template for the game in all the other parts of the world where it was played, and for many other sports. Initially, that stemmed from success on the field as coaches like Jack Gibson and Terry Fearnley imported ideas from American Football, which helped produce a new breed of footballers who starred for the decade's two Kangaroo touring teams as they took Europe by storm in 1982 and 1986. And on the back of that came a new commercialism pioneered by a style of television presentation and marketing which became the envy of British fans as they flocked to buy Aussie jerseys and watch weekly videos flown in from down-under in those days before satellite television.

But the decade started still with plenty of rough edges, never better illustrated than by the "biffo" seen in the inaugural State of Origin matches in Brisbane and Newtown's path to the NSW Grand Final in 1981. State of Origin has gone on to be a juggernaut event in Australia, and its launch on 8th July 1980 was a key moment in the history of the game. Arthur Beetson led Queensland for the first and only time with a team including eight Sydney based players who previously lined up for arch rivals New South Wales, but it was a further two years before the 'Origin' concept was accepted for the full inter-state series. By 1985 it was seen as a 'Holy Grail' for New South Wales when, after Queensland's initial dominance, they won their first Origin series, captained by Steve Mortimer and coached by Terry Fearnley. Despite it battling to halt falling crowds, the

NSW PREMIERSHIP GRAND FINALS
1980 - Canterbury-Banks. 18, beat Eastern Suburbs 4. *(52,881)*
1981 - Parramatta 20, beat Newtown 11. *(57,333)*
1982 - Parramatta 21, beat Manly-Warringah 8. *(52,186)*
1983 - Parramatta 18, beat Manly-Warringah 6. *(40,285)*
1984 - Canterbury-Banks. 6, beat Parramatta 4. *(47,076)*
1985 - Canterbury-Banks. 7, beat St.George 6. *(44,569)*
1986 - Parramatta 4, beat Canterbury-Banks. 2. *(45,843)*
1987 - Manly-Warringah 18, beat Canberra 8. *(50,201)*
1988 - Canterbury-Banks. 24, beat Balmain 12. *(40,000)*
1989 - Canberra 19, beat Balmain 14. *(40,000)*

(Above) One of the most dramatic moments in the history of Australian Rugby League as, on 2nd May 1983, Kevin Humphreys announces his resignation. Seated to his left is Ken Arthurson, and just appearing in the bottom left corner of the picture is Tom Bellew; both of whom would go on to play a major role in the game's recovery and future prosperity. *(Above, right)* English prop Kevin Ward joins with team-mates Ron Gibbs and Darrell Williams as they celebrate Manly's victory in the 1987 Grand Final, the last to be played at the Sydney Cricket Ground as the game moved to the new Sydney Football Stadium in 1988.

game got a major boost in 1982 when Rothmans signed a new three-year naming rights deal which saw the NSW premiership become the Winfield Cup. It was also in 1982 that two new clubs joined the competition, Illawarra (Steelers) and Canberra (Raiders) expanding the boundaries outside Sydney. In contrast, foundation club Newtown (who had been Grand Finalists in 1981) were not invited to take part in 1984 - the same fate hovered over Western Suburbs before they won a court battle to maintain their status.

The Australian League's administration underwent dramatic upheaval in 1983 following the resignation of NSWRL president and executive director Kevin Humphreys, in the face of a television investigation discussing a corruption case in 1977. That led to a new approach to the game's administration, with Ken Arthurson and Tom Bellew heading a more open regime which appointed former international forward John Quayle as the general manager of the NSWRL in July 1983. Quayle was a progressive and visonary leader for the game throughout the rest of the decade, and it was his personal contacts which led to the ground-breaking television commericial fetauring Tina Turner which sent the game soaring to new heights in 1989. That was a year after three more new clubs, Brisbane Broncos, Newcastle Knights and Gold Coast Giants, had joined the competition, and in 1989 Canberra became the first team to take the premiership out of Sydney.

(Above)
Mal Meninga is overcome by emotion as his Souths team won the Brisbane Grand Final in 1985, beating Wynnum-Manly. Hooker Eddie Muller is the Magpies number 12.

(Right)
By the end of the decade this was the face of Rugby League in Australia. Tina Turner with boys in speedos (Allan Langer, 'E.T.' and Wayne Pearce) as the ground-breaking advertising campaign became the talk of sport worldwide.

BRISBANE PREMIERSHIP WINNERS

1980 - Northern Suburbs
1981 - Southern Suburbs
1982 - Wynnum-Manly
1983 - Eastern Suburbs
1984 - Wynnum-Manly
1985 - Southern Suburbs
1986 - Wynnum-Manly
1987 - Past Brothers
1988 - Seagulls-Diehards *
1989 - Valleys
(New name of Valleys)*

THE GAME IN FRANCE

The 1980s was the decade when things started to go wrong for Rugby League in France as the game suffered some very serious blows from which, ever since, it has struggled to recover. Sadly, most of those blows were self inflicted as the French game endured several moments of madness and mayhem, interspersed with their customary - but now much rarer - flashes of magic. Yet the decade started so promisingly when France, with the memory of their triumph over Australia in 1978 still fresh, achieved a drawn series with New Zealand in 1980 as their prestige in the eyes of the French media was on a high and optimism grew ahead of their tour down-under in 1981 - the 'tricolours' first full southern hemisphere tour since 1964. Then came a hammer-blow when, just days after scoring all three of his country's tries against the Kiwis in late 1980, the superstar of French Rugby League Jean-Marc Bourret announced he was signing for the Perpignan Rugby Union club. It was a reminder of the power of the supposedly 'amateur' Union game in France as it rode roughshod over the so-called 'protocol' agreement between the two codes.

(Above)
Joel Roosebrouck, an inspiring captain for France, leading them from the front in a victory over Wales in 1980. Ivan Greseque is in the background.

Much worse was to follow as the 1981 Championship Final, between *X111 Catalan* and Villeneuve, erupted into a wild brawl and was officially abandoned after just four minutes. There had been much controversy over the behaviour of the Catalan players and officials in the lead up to that Final and, facing the wrath of an angry crowd in the Toulouse Stadium, the Federation President, Moniseur René Mauries, resigned and walked away from the game forever. Pictures of the brawl were gleefully transmitted by television stations around the world and, from that moment on, Rugby League was blackballed by the national media in France. The 1981 Cup Final was not played, and the French touring team, captained by the admirable loose-forward from Villeneuve Joel Roosebrouck, who had earlier led them to the European Championship with victories over England and Wales, endured a tough time in the southern hemisphere despite being

CHAMPIONSHIP FINALS

1980 - Villeneuve 12, beat St.Esteve 7.
1981 - Villeneuve-X111 Catalan abandoned.
1982 - X111 Catalan 21, beat St.Esteve 6.
1983 - X111 Catalan 10, beat Villeneuve 8.
1984 - X111 Catalan 30, beat Villeneuve 6.
1985 - X111 Catalan 26, beat Le Pontet 6.
1986 - Le Pontet 19, beat X111 Catalan 6.
1987 - X111 Catalan 11, beat Le Pontet 3.
1988 - Le Pontet 14, beat X111 Catalan 2.
1989 - St.Esteve 23, beat Le Pontet 4.
(The 1981 Championship title not awarded).
All the above Championship Finals played at Toulouse, except 1989 at Narbonne.

(Above) Guy Laforgue playing for Europe in the 50th anniversary match in Paris in 1984.

LORD DERBY CUP FINALS

1980 - X111 Catalan 18, beat Carcassonne 8.
1981 - Carcassonne-X111 Catalan not played.
1982 - Avignon 18, beat Carcassonne 12.
1983 - Carcassonne 10, beat X111 Catalan 3.
1984 - Villeneuve 18, beat Limoux 7.
1985 - X111 Catalan 24, beat Limoux 7.
1986 - Le Pontet 35, beat St.Esteve 10.
1987 - St.Esteve 20, beat X111 Catalan 10.
1988 - Le Pontet 5, beat St.Esteve 2.
1989 - Avignon 12, beat Le Pontet 11.
(The 1981 Cup Final was not played).
All the above Lord Derby Cup Finals played at Narbonne, except 1989 at Albi.

very competitive in New Zealand and the second Test in Australia. The lack of media coverage, most especially on television, has had a massively damaging impact on the game in France ever since those moments of madness in the Toulouse Stadium in May 1981. A further self-inflicted body-blow came early in 1987 when the then Federation President, Jacques Soppelsa, was thrown out in mid-term with the game facing a monetary and moral crisis. Both the Australian and British Rugby Leagues came to the financial rescue, but the French team were unable to undertake their southern hemisphere fixtures in the World Cup which was ongoing at that time. Soppelsa was an academic at the Sorbonne University in Paris and, despite his fall out with the clubs and grassroots officials in the south, he was the man who successfully undertook a campaign to have the French governement restore the name 'rugby' to the game instead of the disdainful 'Jeu a X111.'

In 1984 the French Federation suffered another public relations disaster when their 50th anniversary celebration match, staged in Paris between teams representing Europe and Oceania, was played on a totally unsuitable pitch in front of just a handful of spectators. By this time the Australian influence on the French was becoming significant, with an influx of Aussie players joining their clubs in what turned from an intial trickle in the early 'eighties to an orchestrated campaign, organised largely by Hubie Abbott and Tas Baitieri (pioneers at Albi and Paris Chatillon respectively). Baitieri would become an enormously influentual figure in the French game, and was appointed to be the national team's first overseas coach in 1985 (whilst in his twenties and still a club player). Tas lost that job in 1987 when Soppelsa was forced out of the President's chair, but he later became the Australian Rugby League's man in France as they desperately tried to help the French game stay alive.

Domestically, following the nightmare of 1981, the X111 Catalan club were hit by sanctions and suspensions, but came back to win the Championship in 1982 and embark on a run of four consecutive titles. In fact the Perpignan side played in seven successive Championship Finals from 1982 to '88. Their dominace was eventually broken by the emergence of a new 'super power' in the French game, Le Pontet - an industrial satellite town close to the historic splendour of Avignon in the Provence region. Le Pontet's President, Alain Courtade, was also the town's mayor, so the Rugby League club had lots of cash with which they recruited top players with the promise of lucrative fees and secure jobs. Among those who helped Le Pontet to two titles, and the coveted Cup and Championship 'double' in 1986, were internationals Marc Palanque (signed from Carcassonne) and Christian Macalli (from Villeneuve) alongside overseas imports including Englishman Tim Wilby and Australians John Maguire and Matthew Elliott (who went on to coach Bradford). But the Le Pontet juggernaut exploded spectacularly after the 1989 Championship Final in which some of their players assaulted the referee, Francis Desplas. Duly sanctioned by the Federation, the Le Pontet President refused to accept his club's punishment and declared that his team were pulling out of the League and going to Rugby Union. It was another hammer blow for the 13-aside code.

One of Le Pontet's products had been the teenage prodigy, centre David Fraisse, who made his Test debut aged 17 in 1987. Fraisse stayed in Rugby League with Carcassonne after Le Pontet's demise, and managed to overcome serious injuries sustained in a motorbike accident to become one of a crop of talented young French internationals who emerged during the second half of the decade - among them Gilles Dumas, Patrick Entat and Jacques Moliner - who wore the now (alas) changing tricolour jersey with great distinction as they battled to keep the *treiziste* flame alive in difficult times.

(*Above*)
Tas Baitieri as French coach in 1986, after a 10-all draw with Great Britain in Avignon.

(*Above*)
Second-rower Marc Palanque playing for France against Great Britain in 1986, with support from fellow Le Pontet men Thierry Bernabé and Didier Couston (the latter scorer of a hat-trick in France's win over the British at Perpignan in 1985.) Palanque ran the full gauntlet of French Rugby League in the 'eighties - a Cup winner with Carcassonne in 1983, key man in the glory days of Le Pontet, and captain of his country but also a central figure in the ugly events which led to Le Pontet disappearing in 1989.

THE AMATEUR GAME

(Above) **BARLA internationals on duty for Great Britain during the 1980s.** *(Left)* **Winger Alan Swift, from St.Helens, versus France at Whitehaven in 1982.** *(Middle)* **On attack versus the New Zealand Maori at Hull in 1983.** *(Right)* **Garry Schofield leads the 1983 Young Lions against the Junior Kiwis at Auckland's Carlaw Park. The three British players in the background - Gary Divorty, Deryck Fox and Mike Ford - all joined Schofield in later becoming full Great Britain Test caps in the professional game.**

(Above)
Dave O'Connor, one of the finest amateur players of the decade, in action for Great Britain against the New Zealand Maori in 1983. The Maori hooker tackling him is Trevor Clark. O'Connor was the only man to be BARLA player-of-the-year three times, in 1981, '83 and '84, before he was seriously injured in France in 1987.

Amateur Rugby League enjoyed some heady times throughout the 1980s, as great progress was made in developing competitions and expanding participation domestically whilst, at the same time, more international challenges were enjoyed by Britain's amateur players. It was a decade when the British Amateur Rugby League Association (BARLA) were able to reap the benefits of all their hard work which had galvanized the amateur game since their formation in 1973. At BARLA's birth they began with a membership of just 155 teams; in 1982 they could claim a staggering increase to 700 teams and 18,000 registered players which, by the end of the decade had risen further to 1,100 teams. BARLA's National Cup had become such an attraction for amateur clubs that by 1986 a record number of 164 teams entered the competition, a figure which had increased by the end of the decade to 221 teams. The National Cup had nine different winning clubs during the 1980s, as the competition attracted presitgious sponsorship from the Whitbread company and later British Nuclear Fuels Limited.

Still on the domestic front, BARLA launched their long awaited elite 'National League' in 1986, including ten of the best amateur clubs in the country who all had to fulfil stringent conditions to gain membership. The ten pioneering clubs of the 'National Amateur Rugby League' were: Dudley Hill (Bradford), Egremont (Cumbria), Heworth (York), Leigh Miners, Milford (Leeds), Millom (Cumbria), Pilkington Recs. (St.Helens), Wigan St.Patrick's, West Hull and Woolston (Warrington). The inaugral winners in 1986-87 were Heworth from the city of York, and within three years the 'National League' was extended to 22 clubs and two divisions. The amateur game also made unprecedented progress in other parts of the country well away from BARLA's traditional areas in Yorkshire, Lancashire and Cumbria - the Welsh Amateur Rugby League Association was founded in 1983 to be followed two years later by associations in the Midlands & South West and the North East of England. Many of these developments were helped significantly by *'Open Rugby'* magazine, as were some long awaited breakthroughs which would, eventually, see amateur Rugby League be played in the Armed Forces and the

(Left) **The Great Britain Amateur open-age team pictured at Carnegie College as they prepared to play the New Zealand Maori touring team in November 1983. Left to right:** *(Back row):* **G.Southward (physio), M.Fairbank, A.Brown, J.McGowan, M.Collinson, M.Hough, S.Fallon, A.Hepworth (coach).** *(Middle row):* **M.Doyle (trainer), M.O'Gorman, A.Wheeler, D.O'Connor, C.Andrews, A.Bailey, S.Critchenson, M.Smith, C.Adams (equipment).** *(Front row):* **S.Hulme, M.Amor, A.Diskin, H.Swift (manager), J.Bawden (captain) R.Oldfield (manager), P.Denman, G.Goligy and G.Shaw.**

Rugby Union forced to end their banning of amateur R.L. players. The decade also saw more leaps forward by the Student game, particular milestones being the launch of the Varsity match between Oxford and Cambridge in 1981 and the first Student World Cup staged in New Zealand in 1986. Three years later a second World Cup was a joyous event staged in England.

Amateur Rugby League players were able to enjoy more international experiences than ever throughout the 1980s - as well as their annual games against France at both open-age and youth levels, BARLA sent their second touring team to Papua New Guinea and Australia in 1982, which was followed by another tour in 1986 to Australia. Meanwhile at youth level the BARLA Young Lions toured New Zealand in 1983 and Australia in 1989. The 1983 side, captained by Garry Schofield, was full of very talented players who went on to make massive impressions in the professional game. BARLA hosted in-coming tours from a very powerful New Zealand Maori team in 1983 and also entertained Papua New Guinea in 1987 when they visited Britain and played professional opposition under the auspices of the RFL. At Youth level, BARLA hosted the Australian Schoolboys in 1980 and 1986, and the New Zealand Junior Kiwis in 1987. Working in conjunction with the Sports Council, BARLA were able to make the very significant move of appointing a full-time Director of Coaching in 1982, with Phil Larder taking the post. This was followed in 1988 when the game's first National Development Officer role was created under BARLA's roof. With amateur clubs back in the Challenge Cup in 1986, after a gap of five years, the rising standards of the amateur game were plain to see in what was a golden decade for BARLA and the amateur game as a whole, as Rugby League spread its wings.

(Above) **Garry Schofield, captain of Hunslet Parkside, after winning the BARLA National Youth Cup in 1983.**

BRITISH AMATEUR RUGBY LEAGUE NATIONAL CUP FINALS

Open Age
1980 - Pilkington Recs. 16, Dewsbury Celtic 5.
1981 - Beecroft & Wightman 11, Lock Lane 2.
1982 - Pilkington Recs. 19, Milford 2.
1983 - Leigh Miners 12, Lock Lane 8.
1984 - Dudley Hill 24, Mysons 16.
1985 - Jubilee 26, West Hull 10.
1986 - Mysons 17, Millom 8.
1987 - Thatto Heath 15, Heworth 8.
1988 - Wigan St.Patrick's 28, Elland 8.
1989 - Crosfields 25, Kells 11.

Youth (Under-19)
1980 - Wigan St.Patrick's 33, Redhill 0.
1981 - Wigan St.Patrick's 16, Rosebridge 11.
1982 - Wigan St.Patrick's 21, St.John Fisher 10.
1983 - Hunslet Parkside 27, Kells 2.
1984 - Leigh Miners 22, Kells 14.
1985 - Wigan St.Patrick's 16, Leigh Miners 6.
1986 - West Hull 21, Villa Youth Club 9.
1987 - Wigan St.Patrick's 17, Ellenborough 12.
1988 - Leigh Miners 50, Ellenborough 8.
1989 - Widnes Tigers 39, Kells 16.

THE FINAL WHISTLE

I hope you have enjoyed this look back at the 1980s, although you might share my frustration that we just haven't got enough space to cover in detail all the things which made this such an incredible decade for Rugby League. Nevertheless, this fifth volume in our history series should have given all readers a reminder of some of the players, teams and famous events that shaped the game in the 'eighties and sent it surging ahead with such optimism into the 'nineties.

Throughout the 1980s I published *'Open Rugby'* magazine and was proud to be able to help many initiatives which promoted the development of the game - these included helping amateur clubs and leagues set up in new areas, the 'British Upper Schools & Colleges' Association, the 'Freedom in Rugby Campaign' which tried to break down the Rugby Union's barrier to amateur League players, and taking the initial steps to help members of the Armed Services get the opportunity to organise games. At the highest level of the professional game, I was delighted to be able to create the Golden Boot award for the world's top player and help in the planning of a World Club

Challenge (initially in discussions with the Canterbury-Bankstown boss Peter Moore) which would eventually lead to the famous Wigan versus Manly match at Central Park in 1987. Designing and producing the poster for that game, featuring 'Rambo' Ronnie Gibbs, was a pleasure, and came a year after doing a similar poster for Wigan to promote their staging the opening fixture of the 1986 Kangaroo tour. Further afield on the international front were attempts to take the game across new frontiers by helping Italian Mario Majone organise the Great Britain-France match in Venice in 1982, and Mike Mayer his now rather infamous Wigan-Warrington challenge match in Milwaukee in 1989. Truly the 'eighties was a decade where a spirit of adventure prevailed. Nothing ventured, nothing gained.

But being able to help in all such initiatives was dependent on having the right vehicle to promote and inform, so it was essential that

(Above)
Andrew Varley in 1984 after receiving the Rugby League 'photographer of the year award'. And the front cover of the last but one edition of the 'eighties of *'Open Rugby'* featuring the Sheffield Eagles.

the magazine came out every month, as it did throughout the decade. And it was my aim to make that magazine look good and present Rugby League in an attractive and visually exciting fashion - which meant we needed good photographs. That's where my friend Andrew Varley came into the picture as *'Open Rugby's'* chief photographer from 1980 onwards, and very rapidly became recognised as the Rugby League's leading 'snapper'. I mention Andrew because a large number of the pictures you will see in this book are the ones he submitted to *'Open Rugby'* throughout the 1980s, and I am very grateful to him for helping provide such a fine visual record of the decade.

During the latter years of the 'eighties Rugby League really was enjoying a boom time, and I like to think our magazine reflected that. The front cover illustrated on this page was one of my favourites, it was the November 1989 issue, and featured Mark Aston of Sheffield as we reported on the Eagles attracting over 8,500 fans to their game vesus Widnes, who had just beaten Canberra to be crowned world club champions, whilst at the same time we were covering the Kiwis on tour. As the decade came to a close, our very respected columnist Paul Fitzpatrick of *'The Guardian'* asked the question "How will the 'eighties be judged? As one of the game's Golden Ages, or as a time of lost opportunity?" Some 25 years on since the end of that decade, I have to say, truly, I think it was both.

Harry Edgar (Editor - 'Rugby League Journal')